Zhu Xi

Zhu Xi BASIC TEACHINGS

Translated by
DANIEL K. GARDNER

Columbia University Press

Columbia University Press
Publishers Since 1893
New York   Chichester, West Sussex
cup.columbia.edu

Library of Congress Cataloging-in-Publication Data
Names: Zhu, Xi, 1130–1200. author. | Gardner,
    Daniel K., 1950– translator.
Title: Zhu xi : basic teachings / translated by Daniel K.
    Gardner.
Other titles: Zhuzi yu lei. Selections. English
Description: New York : Columbia University Press,
    [2022] | Includes bibliographical references and index.
Identifiers: LCCN 2022002016 (print) |
    LCCN 2022002017 (ebook) | ISBN 9780231206327
    (hardback) | ISBN 9780231206334 (trade paperback) |
    ISBN 9780231556422 (ebook)
Subjects: LCSH: Philosophy—Early works to 1800.
Classification: LCC B128.C52 E5 2022 (print) |
    LCC B128.C52 (ebook) | DDC 181/.11—dc23/
    eng/20220308
LC record available at https://lccn.loc.gov/2022002016
LC ebook record available at https://lccn.loc.gov
    /2022002017

Columbia University Press books are printed on
permanent and durable acid-free paper.
Printed in the United States of America

Cover image: Detail of rubbing from "Wu Family Shrines"
    pictorial stones, 25–220 C.E.

Contents

Introduction

Zhu Xi 朱熹 (1130–1200) would rank at the top of any list of the most influential people in China's history. For seven hundred years, from the thirteenth century to the early years of the twentieth, his particular version of the Confucian tradition was the one the political and intellectual elite regarded as "orthodox."* School children would study, indeed memorize line-by-line, the four texts in the Confucian canon that he believed constituted the core curriculum. And with those texts, they would read, and memorize, Zhu Xi's detailed interlinear commentaries on each, as these interpretations were expected to guide their reading and shape their understanding of Confucian beliefs and practices.

Given the growing prominence of his teachings, in 1313, the Chinese state designated these four texts, known now simply as the Four Books, and Zhu Xi's accompanying interlinear commentary on them, as the core texts of the influential civil service examination system. Candidates hoping to succeed in the examinations and gain official positions were required to memorize

---

*Called *Daoxue* 道學, literally "Learning of the Way." This book uses the conventional English name of Neo-Confucianism for Zhu Xi's school of Confucianism.

and demonstrate mastery of these Four Books, as well as Zhu Xi's interpretation of them. It was thus supposed that Zhu Xi's teachings and commentaries on the dominant Confucian tradition would guide the imperial government and its officials in the administration of the Chinese realm.

Zhu Xi was born in 1130 in Youqi County in Fujian Province, shortly after the great crisis of the Song dynasty (960–1279)—the conquest of north China by the Jurchen people and the flight of the Song court to the south in 1127. His father, Zhu Song 朱松 (1097–1143), had moved the family to Fujian from Wuyuan County, Jiangxi, to take up the post of district sheriff. Zhu's early schooling was at home, under the supervision of his father. When Zhu Song died in 1143, the education of young Zhu fell to three of his father's acquaintances, an arrangement made by Zhu Song on his deathbed. Later in life Zhu Xi would remark that the three men were fond not only of Confucian teachings but of Buddhist teachings as well. We do not learn from him which Buddhist texts or teachings in particular he might have encountered, but he does tell us that at this time he frequented Buddhist and Daoist schools. His fascination with Buddhism continued for the next ten years or so.

The person credited with showing Zhu the error of Buddhist ways and bringing him firmly into the Confucian fold is Li Tong 李侗 (1093–1163). Li had studied under Luo Congyan 羅從彥 (1072–1135), a disciple of Yang Shi 楊時 (1053–1135), who, in turn, had studied under Cheng Yi 程頤 (1033–1107), regarded by Zhu as one of the four great Neo-Confucian thinkers of the Northern Song period (960–1127). Given this line of transmission, Zhu would claim that he had studied indirectly under Cheng Yi and considered him to be his spiritual master.

By 1148, Zhu Xi had already demonstrated his intellectual precociousness, having won the *jinshi* degree, the highest degree in the country's competitive civil service examinations, at the age of nineteen (the average age of successful *jinshi* candidates at this time was mid-thirties). Success in the examinations led to his first official posting in 1153 as subprefectural registrar of Tongan county in Fujian, a position he held through 1156. There, his biography tells us, he supervised the local registrars, promoted education, built a library, strengthened city defenses, and reported on public morality. Upon leaving his post in Tongan, for the next twenty years he declined requests to serve in office. Instead he took up temple guardianships; these low-paying sinecurial posts enabled him to eke out a living while writing, teaching, and meeting with prominent thinkers of the day, such as Lü Zuqian 呂祖謙 (1137–1181), Zhang Shi 張栻 (1130–1180), and Lu Jiuyuan 陸九淵 (1139–1193).

In 1179, Zhu Xi accepted an appointment as prefect of Nan-kang County in Jiangxi. There, we are told, he continued his commitment to promoting education, evidenced perhaps most clearly by his efforts to revive the famous White Deer Grotto Academy, originally founded in the late tenth century. The "Articles of Learning" he compiled for the academy reflect his devotion to learning for the sake of moral improvement, not as a means to worldly success. These "Articles" would be extremely influential, serving as a model for academies throughout much of East Asia and into the twentieth century. Zhu's term at Nankang expired in 1181. He did accept further appointments as prefect of Zhangzhou in Fujian in 1190 and prefect of Tanzhou in 1194 but held each of these for less than a year. In total, Zhu Xi served in public office for only nine or so years, far fewer than might be expected of a man who lived for more than fifty years after receiving the prestigious *jinshi* degree.[1]

Zhu may have not dedicated his life to holding office, but his keen interest in the political order cannot be questioned. Not only did he acquit himself with distinction in the offices he did hold, but he also engaged directly in contemporary political discourse: he submitted a number of sealed memorials to the throne (in 1162, 1180, 1188) and even went to the capital for personal audiences with the emperor (in 1163, 1181, 1188). And, in late 1194 he served briefly as lecturer-in-waiting at court, where he lectured Emperor Ningzong on the short Confucian classic, the *Greater Learning* (*Daxue* 大學).

Certain themes run through these memorials and audiences: the emperor, Zhu urged, must rectify his mind if the empire is to become tranquil and orderly; the military must be strengthened if the central plain—the traditional heartland of Chinese civilization, now under the control of the Jurchen Jin (1115–1234)—is to be recovered; and the emperor must establish sound and effective personnel policies and select only worthy and talented men for government service.

Still, teaching and writing were clearly dearest to Zhu Xi. In surveying the Chinese world of the twelfth century, he saw a country and a culture in crisis. The Confucian Way of the past was in decline. His hope was that through teaching and writing he might help restore this Way and ensure its transmission to later generations.

Since the beginning of the Song, foreigners had occupied territory traditionally belonging to the Chinese. First, in the midtenth century the Khitan tribespeople from Mongolia extended their control over sixteen northern prefectures surrounding Beijing. In the early years of the twelfth century the Jurchen tribes of Manchuria in turn extinguished Khitan power; but, not content with the northern prefectures of the Khitan alone, Jurchen forces continued south, eventually taking all of north China and establishing their own Jin dynasty there. Henceforth, from 1125 until the fall of the dynasty in 1279, Song control over China was limited to the area south of the Huai River. Zhu, along with other officials of the Southern Song, expressed displeasure with this occupation of the north and, even more, with the government's decision during 1141 and 1142 to sue for peace with the Jurchen rather than to fight for repossession of land that was rightfully Chinese. His opposition would put him at odds with some of the most powerful officials at the court.

For Zhu, occupation of the north did not represent just a political and territorial threat to the Chinese people but a moral and cultural threat as well. Zhu shared the Confucian assumption that, when the true Way prevailed in China, those who came into contact with it would recognize its moral power and readily submit to it. That the Jurchen had in fact not submitted, but rather had thoroughly overrun north China, establishing their own rule over what had been Chinese territory, indicated that the great Way—the Way that set the Chinese apart from all other people—had all but disappeared in the Central Plain, the heartland of Chinese civilization. The question posed by the "barbarian" subjugation of the north, then, was not simply how to strengthen China's military forces but how to reinvigorate a greatly weakened cultural and moral tradition.

If the Way was in decline, much of the responsibility, Zhu maintained, fell on the shoulders of the emperor and the ruling elite. In memorials to the emperor and letters to acquaintances he berated rulers and the bureaucracy for their moral turpitude. And his refusals to accept offers of official position were often cast in the form of protest against a corrupt and immoral government. But as severe as he found some the ills of government to be, the cure for them, he was convinced, remained simple (and very much in accord with traditional Confucian beliefs): the ruler merely had to rectify himself. Once the ruler became rectified, his moral charisma would inspire those around him to follow his moral example. They, in turn, would move others to the same course, until the entire realm achieved moral perfection and the great Way again prevailed.[2]

The continued popularity of Buddhist teachings was further evidence for Zhu that the times were out of joint. The Confucian Way had been losing ground to Buddhism, especially to Chan teachings. Zhu himself knew that these teachings were seductive, because, after all, he himself had engaged in study of them for more than ten years, beginning at age fifteen or sixteen. His writings and conversations evince a clear fear of Buddhism's allure for people of the day: "Be they adults or children, officials, farmers, or merchants, men or women, all enter the Buddhists gates."[3] He once remarked that although families might have the wherewithal to resist Buddhist teachings for a generation or two, after the third generation they were sure to be converted to them.[4] What especially worried Zhu Xi was the appeal Buddhist teachings had to the intelligentsia.[5] These were the men he counted on to keep the Confucian Way alive and well. If they surrendered to the foreign creed, whom could he depend on? "In the world there are but a few great men, and they have all been drawn into Buddhism—how detrimental!"[6] So attractive had Buddhism become that even disciples of the great Cheng Yi and his brother Cheng Hao 程顥 (1032–1085) had turned to it.[7]

Zhu Xi was most critical of Buddhism where Confucians had long been critical. To his mind, Buddhism's search for personal enlightenment promoted self-interest and undermined the long-standing normative five relationships of Chinese society—ruler and subject, parent and child, husband and wife, elder brother and younger brother, and friend and friend. Additionally, in its belief that things have no abiding nature and that the world as we tend to view it is illusory, Buddhism reduces everything to empty annihilation. For Zhu Xi, of course, the world as we see it is indeed very real and the Confucian imperative is to serve it and improve it.

Furthermore, the so-called Confucian learning of the day was not the right sort. Many of Zhu's conversations with students read as harsh indictments of the contemporary learning pursued by Confucians. To him their learning was nothing like that promoted by the great sages of the past. According to Zhu, the sages had taken as the express aim of learning "to understand moral principle clearly in order that one might cultivate one's person, and thereafter extend that perfection to others."[8] Drawing on the *Analects* (*Lunyu* 論語), Zhu described this sort of learning as "learning for one's own sake" (為己之學).[9] But contemporary students seemed to have abandoned this sort of learning completely as they scrambled to achieve far less noble goals: reputation for profound thinking, literary renown, and wealth and official rank. They were engaged in what Confucius, and now Zhu Xi, called "learning for the sake of others" (為人之學).

Ironically, the gravest contemporary threat to true learning was posed by the very system meant to ensure the propagation of Confucian learning: the civil service examinations. The prospects for worldly success that they offered—prestige, official status, power, and great wealth—diverted students from the real aim of learning, "learning for the sake of one's self." Zhu Xi would write, "Today's students covet wealth and office, not the Way and righteousness. They want to be become men of high position, not good men."[10] While he welcomed the examination system as a reasonable means of recruiting capable officials, he felt strongly that the intense competition it bred had created an atmosphere in which students gave imbalanced attention to "learning for the examination," all but abandoning "learning for one's own sake."

In Zhu Xi's eyes, then, the Way was in decline and customs had degenerated. The Confucian learning of the day, tilted so heavily toward examination and worldly success, had not only failed to solve the problems confronting society but also had become a problem itself. Yet, as discouraged as he was about the state of learning he found around him, Zhu never lost faith that ultimately, through education and learning, the Way would be restored and the tradition revived.

To restore the Way in crisis Zhu Xi dove deeply into the writings of the sages and worthies of the past. His life from 1160 until his death was dedicated to reflecting on the Thirteen Classics that constituted the Confucian canon, searching them for the dominant threads that gave abiding meaning and coherence to the Confucian tradition. The reader will see, in the translation that follows, that Zhu frequently based his arguments on his explication of passages from the Classics. He was aided in his deep reflection on the canon by the teachings of four Northern Song thinkers, in particular—Zhou Dunyi 周敦頤 (1017–1073), Zhang Zai 張載 (1020–1077), and the Cheng brothers, Hao and Yi. The writings and records of conversations of these near-contemporaries would be a constant source of inspiration for Zhu Xi and did much to color his own reflection on the meaning of the canon. Indeed, Zhu's philosophical system is often characterized as an elaborate synthesis of the Confucian tradition, from the teachings of the sages and worthies of distant antiquity through those of his Neo-Confucian predecessors in the Northern Song.

If resuscitation of Confucianism was the purpose behind his lifelong reflection, it has to be said that this reflection reformulated rather than resuscitated. The philosophical system that resulted from Zhu's immersive reflection on the past represents, in fact, a major reshaping of the tradition. Perhaps most significantly, Zhu Xi argued for a change in the Confucian school's "core curriculum." For more than a millennium, since the Han dynasty (202 BCE–220 CE), the so-called Five Classics—the *Book of Changes* (*Yijing* 易經), the *Classic of Odes* (*Shijing* 詩經), the

Classic of History (*Shujing* 書經), the *Book of Rites* (*Liji* 禮記), and the *Spring and Autumn Annals* (*Chunqiu* 春秋)—had been *the* authoritative texts in the Confucian tradition, the texts to be read before all others. This was the set of texts to be mastered by those competing in the civil service examinations. As Zhu Xi reflected on the canon, however, he found greater inspiration elsewhere. To be sure, the Five Classics, in his treatment, remained canonical— he wrote commentaries and essays on all of them—but Zhu believed that they did not capture the central message of the Confucian school as well as other texts in the canon did, especially the *Greater Learning*, the *Analects*, the *Mencius* (*Mengzi* 孟子), and the *Mean* (*Zhongyong* 中庸). The *Greater Learning* and the *Mean*, originally chapters in the *Book of Rites*, had by the late eleventh century begun circulating as independent texts. In 1190 Zhu Xi published these four texts as a collection for the first time, together with his interlinear commentaries on them, under the title the *Four Masters* (*Sizi* 四子). And in 1313, the Chinese state declared these four texts, known by then as the Four Books (*Sishu* 四書), together with Zhu Xi's commentaries, to be the core texts of the civil service examination. The Four Books thus displaced the Five Classics as the authoritative texts in the Confucian tradition; they retained their privileged status in Chinese society through the early years of the twentieth century.

This shift to the Four Books marks an "inward" shift in the Confucian tradition. Although the Five Classics and the Four Books share a fundamental moral, social, and political vision, the two collections emphasize different parts of that vision. Interested mainly in human moral behavior in practice, the Five Classics illustrate Confucian moral virtues using specific examples and lessons from history; lay out ideal institutions and methods of governance drawn from the past; describe in detail how one should conduct oneself in various, concrete life situations; and prescribe the ritual practices essential to the maintenance of a well-ordered society. From these texts the ruler learns how to rule, the minister learns how to administer the realm, father and mother learn how to parent, children learn how to express filial devotion, older and younger learn how to show mutual respect, and friends learn how to be friends. The Four Books tend to be less historical and less concrete. Concerned more with the inner realm of human morality, they deal with abstract matters like the nature of human beings, the springs or inner source of their morality, their path to moral self-realization, and their relationship to the cosmos.[11]

That such texts in the canon should appeal to Confucian thinkers in the Song is not surprising. By the late Tang and early Song, Confucian scholars had been compelled to ask new kinds of questions—partly as a result of the sorts of metaphysical questions being raised by Daoist and Buddhist thinkers. No longer could they restrict their interests to human relationships and the sociopolitical realm. The prevailing intellectual concerns of the day required that they reflect on matters of human nature, the mind and self-realization, and the place of human beings in the universe. As Confucian thinkers like Zhu Xi looked to their canon for inspiration, they found in the Four Books in particular texts deeply resonant with their philosophical interests. And Zhu's early study of Buddhist teachings may well have made him more open and receptive to the "inward" message these texts offered.

If this curricular shift represents a reshaping of the Confucian tradition, so too does the change in philosophical language and terminology that accompanies it. Zhu Xi, drawing on his Northern Song predecessors, places the moral predicament human beings face in a language of metaphysics that little resembles the language of classical Confucian thinkers like Confucius, Mencius, and Xunzi. But that language would not be unfamiliar to Song intellectuals, who had begun to analyze and describe the world around them—and the moral mission of human beings in it—in terms of *li* 理, "principle," and *qi* 氣, "psychophysical stuff."

Zhu explains that all things and affairs in the universe are possessed of principle, which he defines as both the reason why a thing is as it is and the rule to which a thing should conform. In human beings, this principle is identical to their originally good nature. The originally good nature, as the principle of humanity, is the same in all people. But every thing and every person is also born with an endowment of psychophysical stuff, the quantity and quality of which differs from one thing and one person to the other. Some stuff is purer than others, some clearer, some less dense, some less turbid, and so on. This endowment of psychophysical stuff accounts for individuation in things and in people. And not just physical individuation, but mental and moral as well. Our particular endowment of psychophysical stuff, depending on its clarity, density, and so forth, can permit our principle—which is one with our benevolent human nature—to become manifest. Or, it can obscure principle, preventing it from becoming manifest. The good news, in Zhu's understanding, is that this endowment of psychophysical stuff can be transformed and refined, enabling us in the end to give realization to our human nature and goodness within. This is where the self-cultivation (*xiushen* 修身) process comes in. By investigating things (*gewu* 格物) and the principle in them—a crucial process in Zhu's program of self-cultivation—human beings can come to understand principle better, and thereby achieve moral perfection.

Arguably, it was by drawing on a language both more contemporary and more meaningful to his Song audience that Zhu was able to make the venerable but stagnant Confucian tradition contemporary and meaningful again. It should be emphasized, though, that by showing the metaphysical possibilities of the long normative texts in the Chinese tradition, Zhu at the same time was giving added—and needed—legitimacy to the newly developing Song system of *li* and *qi* metaphysics. By integrating this metaphysics into his interpretation of the Classics, he brought new life to Confucianism, but he also lent the new metaphysical thinking the authority of the Confucian tradition.

To spread the Way, Zhu wrote prolifically. His most significant and influential writings were his commentaries on each of the Four Books, known together as the *Collected Commentaries on the Four Books* (*Sishu jizhu* 四書集注). It was largely owing to the powerful effect of these interlinear commentaries that the Four Books gained the attention they did and supplanted the Five Classics as the core texts in the tradition. But while elevating the Four Books, Zhu's admiration for the Five Classics never waned. He continued his study of them throughout his life and wrote commentaries on all of them, with the exception of the *Spring and Autumn Annals*. He also wrote a commentary on the *Classic on Filial Piety* (*Xiaojing* 孝經).

History, too, was important. In Zhu's view, it documented the Way in operation. He produced several historical works, one on famous statesmen of the Northern Song period, one on the development of the Cheng brothers' school of Neo-Confucianism, and one a synopsis of the greatest historical work of the Song, Sima Guang's 司馬光 (1019–1086) monumental *Comprehensive Mirror for Aid in Government* (*Zizhi tongjian* 資治通鑑).[12]

And, as part of his mission to transmit the Way, he was also eager to promote the teachings of his predecessors and their Song understanding of the Confucian tradition. He wrote commentaries on some of the most influential works of the Northern Song, and, in particular, Zhou Dunyi's *Diagram of the Great Ultimate* (*Taiji tushuo* 太極圖説) and Zhang Zai's *Western Inscription* (*Ximing* 西銘).[13] With his friend and colleague Lü Zuqian, he compiled an anthology of comments, 622 in all, by those predecessors he most admired—Zhou Dunyi, Zhang Zai, Cheng Hao, and Cheng

Yi—to make their ideas, scattered about in voluminous writings and conversations, as accessible to students as possible. This volume, *Reflection on Things at Hand* (*Jinsi lu* 近思錄), and Zhu's frequently professed admiration for these four men, ensured that history would regard them as Zhu Xi's great intellectual forebears. Finally, he compiled editions of the Cheng brothers' conversations and the conversations of Xie Liangzuo 謝良佐 (1050–1103), a renowned disciple of the Chengs.[14]

Zhu Xi's letters, essays, poetry, postscripts, eulogies, and other prose works, written throughout his life, are found in the one hundred chapters of the *Collected Works of Zhu Xi* (*Zhu Xi ji* 朱熹). All of these texts showcase Zhu the scholar, writer, and editor. The collection titled *Classified Conversations of Master Zhu* (*Zhuzi yulei* 朱子語類) showcases Zhu the teacher. Compiled and edited by Li Jingde 黎靖德 (fl. 1263) in 1270, seventy years after Zhu's death, it comprises 140 chapters of sayings and conversations with his pupils in the period from 1170 to 1200. In these conversations Zhu Xi explains, elaborates, clarifies, revises, and defends his central philosophical teachings; here he reflects widely on the sweep of the Confucian tradition, piecing together from his deep understanding of it a renewed Confucianism he hoped would ensure the Way's transmission well into the future. Remarks made to students in teaching point them—and us—to where he finds the Classics especially inspirational and relevant to the concerns of the day, enabling us to understand better where and how the canonical Confucian texts and his evolving philosophical ideals inform and enrich each other. In making the case to students for the superiority of his philosophical beliefs, he allows the reader today to observe him in ongoing debate with other important thinkers of his day. For all these reasons, the *Classified Conversations of Master Zhu* is the main source for this present book.

The *Classified Conversations* is essential reading for anyone interested in Zhu Xi's thought. It is also lively reading, as we get

to observe Zhu in the act of weaving together from earlier strands
of the Chinese tradition—the Confucian Classics, especially the
Four Books and Five Classics, the writings of the great early
Confucians, the works of Confucians since the ninth century like
Han Yu 韓愈 (768–824), Zhou Dunyi, Zhang Zai, Cheng Hao,
and Cheng Yi, and even Daoist and Buddhist texts—a philosophical system whose authority would now be dominant in China
through the early years of the twentieth century.

Notes on the Text and Translation

Zhu Xi's writings and recorded conversations constitute hundreds of chapters. In translating Zhu Xi into English, the translator must make choices. My choice here has been relatively easy. In "classifying" Zhu Xi's conversations in the *Classified Conversations of Master Zhu*, editor Li Jingde dedicated the first thirteen chapters to conversations explaining Zhu's general philosophical system. Readers there are introduced to his metaphysics of principle (*li*), psychophysical stuff (*qi*), spirit beings (*guishen* 鬼神), human nature (*xing* 性), mind-heart (*xin* 心), and emotions (*qing* 情); and to his program of self-cultivation—that is, the curriculum that Confucians should follow to attain moral perfection. These chapters, to my mind, constitute the best overview of Zhu Xi's basic and most enduring philosophical teachings, and selections from them form the basis of this present volume. Occasionally, I supplement them with passages from the *Collected Works of Zhu Xi* and from Zhu's commentaries on the Confucian Classics.

Li Jingde's 1270 publication of the *Classified Conversations* was based on six earlier published collections of conversations recorded by Zhu's disciples. In categorizing the 140 chapters of conversations into twenty-six general topics, he adopted the organization of Huang Shiyi's 黃士毅 (fl. 1196–1219) earlier collection of Zhu Xi's conversations, published in 1215. The principle of organization in Li's text thus is thematic, with no regard for chronology. As a consequence, a comment on human nature made in 1184, let's say, may follow one made in 1196, yet precede one made in 1178. Each passage in the *Classified Conversations* lists the student-recorder's name, and because the preface to Li's volume provides the years each student studied under Zhu, we can roughly date the passages. Li himself sees no real benefit to providing approximate dates for each passage; neither do I. My selections from the thirteen chapters are presented largely in the order they appear in Li's text, though I do infrequently move a passage from its original spot to another one if its philosophical significance is more clearly highlighted there. Chapter and page number indicating the location in the Chinese text are given for each passage.

Passages in the *Classified Conversations of Master Zhu* take a few different forms. The most common, perhaps, is the teaching or saying by Zhu Xi. In these, there is no mention of an interlocutor. Presumably, these were sayings taken down during or after a lecture by Zhu or during or after a conversation with him. Then there is the "conversation" with Zhu, in which typically an unnamed questioner poses a question and Zhu Xi responds. Last, there is the conversation in which multiple pupils are present, and the original question posed to Zhu is followed up by further questions. Usually, the questioner's name is not recorded. The passage merely says, "someone asked." When the name is recorded, I identify the questioner in a footnote only when he is a person of some note.

Because this is a record of teachings, Zhu typically would be addressing an audience of one or more particular students. We should assume that Zhu, like Confucius in the *Analects*, tailored his remarks to the particular student or group of students with whom he was speaking. His teachings here, then, are what we might call "perspectival," which is to say his response to questions about "reverential attentiveness" or "selfish desires," for example, might be different on different occasions, depending on Zhu's sense of the particular audience and its needs. Some apparent differences or inconsistencies should be expected.

In citing from the works of the Cheng brothers, Zhu sometimes specifies which of the two brothers, Hao or Yi, made the remark. At other times, though, he attributes the remark to "Master Cheng" without specifying the brother. In some instances, it may be that he does not know which brother is the author because the original records available to him provided no indication; in other cases it may be that, in his view, the remark reflects an idea held strongly by both brothers and that "Master Cheng" refers collectively to the brothers Cheng.

I follow the standard practice of providing characters for Chinese terms and names on their first occurrence. I have included a "Glossary of Key Terms" at the back of the book for reference.

As a record of conversations, the language in the *Collected Conversations* is considerably more vernacular and less stylized than what we find in Zhu Xi's *Collected Literary Works* and commentaries on the Classics. This results in occasional difficulty, at least for this translator. At times, the language can be highly idiomatic, drawing on what are perhaps local expressions, and, in any event, not always readily intelligible. Then there are words like "this" and "that," and "here" and "there," whose referents are sometimes unclear because we do not see the gestures that accompanied the words. Nor can a record of conversations always capture the tone and inflection of voice that suggests irony, sarcasm, affirmation, criticism, and the like. These particular challenges aside, I do try to convey in the translation the more leisurely and colloquial tone of Zhu's teachings here.

I base the translation on the Zhonghua shuju edition of the *Zhuzi yulei* published in 1986; I also consulted the Chuanjing tang

傳經堂 edition of 1880, on which, I should note, the Zhonghua shuju edition itself is based. The references that appear at the end of each translated passage are to the Zhonghua shuju edition, simply because it is the most widely available and commonly cited edition of the text. So, taking 9.152 as an example: 9 refers to the chapter or *juan* 卷 number, and 152 to the page number. I have consulted earlier translations found in *Source Book in Chinese Philosophy*, edited by Wing-tsit Chan; *Sources of Chinese Tradition*, edited by Wm. Theodore de Bary; *Zhu Xi: Selected* Writing, edited by Philip Ivanhoe; and *Shushi gorui* 朱子語類 [Classified conversations of Master Zhu], edited by Morohashi Testuji 諸橋轍次 and Yasuoka Masuhiro 安岡正篤. I have previously translated some of the passages here in *Learning to Be a Sage: Selections from Master Chu, Arranged Topically* and in various articles; while I consulted them, I was eager to read the text with a fresh set of eyes and what Zhu called an "open mind."

Zhu Xi

The universe is orderly. Each thing and affair in it has a reason for being and a rule to which it should conform. This Zhu Xi calls *li*, conventionally translated as "principle." The moment a thing comes into existence it is possessed of this principle. "Principle is one, its manifestations are many," says Zhu, following his Northern Song predecessors Zhang Zai and Cheng Yi. Which is to say, although different things in the universe manifest principle in different ways, the rule to which things conform is ultimately one, as is the reason things are as they are. This oneness of principle gives coherence and order to the cosmos and all things in it. Admittedly, the word "principle" does not convey much here, but it can perhaps best be understood as something like a blueprint or pattern for the cosmos, encoded in each and every thing in the universe; each thing has a particular manifestation of this principle, thus designating the more particular role that thing is to play in the coherent, cosmic plan.[1]

But just as all things and affairs are possessed of principle, so all things and affairs are endowed at their inception with an allotment of *qi*, variously translated as "material force," "matter-energy," "vital energy," and "psychophysical stuff." Psychophysical stuff is most fitting, in my view, for it explicitly—even if a bit cumbersomely—conveys the sense that *qi* accounts for both the physical and psychic characteristics of a thing or affair. This psychophysical stuff is dynamic, circulating endlessly, and coalescing in particular configurations to constitute particular things in the universe. Each thing thus receives its own particular endowment of psychophysical stuff, the quality and quantity of which differs. It is this endowment of psychophysical stuff, therefore, that explains the differences among the myriad things in the universe.

A fundamental belief for Zhu, indeed a premise of his entire philosophical system, is that there is nothing in the universe without both principle and psychophysical stuff. The two entities simply cannot exist independently of each other: without principle the psychophysical stuff has no ontological reason for being, and without psychophysical stuff principle has nothing in which to inhere and become manifest. Students are insistent in asking him which of the two exists first. It is a question that cannot be answered, he says; yet, when pushed, he appears to incline in the direction of principle.

Like everything in the universe, heaven and earth are just a matter of principle and psychophysical stuff. They came into existence out of "undifferentiated chaos" only when the principle and psychophysical stuff for heaven and earth came into existence. For Zhu there is no Abrahamic sort of creator deity. Principle and circulating psychophysical stuff spontaneously engender heaven and earth as they do all things and affairs in the universe. And the quality of the stuff heaven and earth each received at the time explains their differences: heaven got the pure and refined psychophysical stuff, while earth got the heavy and turbid stuff. As described by Zhu, heaven is the light, ever-revolving psychophysical stuff; earth is the coarse and compressed stuff within it, at its center.

While the mind-heart of heaven possesses consciousness, Zhu Xi stresses that it does not plan or take deliberate action "the way the human mind-heart does." The mind-heart of heaven, in his words, is *ling* 靈 (meaning "numinous" or "spiritually efficacious"), and it is this quality that directs heaven's activity. Disciples, he says in the *Classified Conversations* (1.5), would be mistaken to think of heaven anthropomorphically, as if a person were sitting there judging human behavior.

Zhu's sustained interest in the operations of heaven, earth, the sun, and the moon, as evidenced in passages here, shows a Confucianism that focuses on the affairs and morality of humankind but insists on viewing them in the context of the cosmos. The scope of inquiry has expanded and is no longer restricted largely to man's relation to man as it had been in the teachings of the classical Confucians. Zhu's serious study of the cosmos can be related in part, no doubt, to his belief that humankind and the cosmos share in the one universal principle. For him, understanding of humankind and understanding of the cosmos would, thus, be mutually illuminating.

In one of the longer chapters in the *Classified Conversations*, Zhu Xi takes up the topic of *guishen*, or spirit beings, and considers how spirit phenomena fit into his worldview. In a sense, he is compelled to comment on them. Confucian Classics like the *Book of Rites*, the *Zuo Commentary*, the *Book of Changes*, and the *Mean* all claim that spirit beings exist. And, in twelfth-century China, signs of ghosts, spirits, and gods appear everywhere around him: temples and shrines to powerful deities dot the landscape, tales of ghosts and monsters circulate widely, freak accidents and miracles are commonplace, spirit possession is rampant, and divination is part and parcel of daily life.[2] Unsurprisingly, Zhu's students are keen to hear their master's views on spirits, and repeatedly ask him about the existence of spirit beings and how they can be explained.

In the *Classified Conversations*, Zhu understands spirit beings to be of three distinct types: (1) the expansion and contraction of *yin* 陰 and *yang* 陽, as manifested in natural phenomena such as wind and rain, thunder and lightning, day and night; (2) beings such as ghosts, monsters, and demons, who at times appear before humankind; and (3) ancestral spirits, the recipients of ancestral sacrifice. Like all other things in the universe, they can be explained in terms of principle and a particular allotment of psychophysical stuff. With such explanation, Zhu Xi integrates spirit beings fully into our understandable world, and makes them a "natural," even if an occasionally strange, unusual, or even freakish, part of it.

A. Principle (*Li*) and Psychophysical Stuff (*Qi*)

1. Someone asked: Yesterday, didn't you say that before heaven and earth exist, there first exists principle?

Zhu replied: Before heaven and earth exist, there is but principle. Once this principle exists, heaven and earth exist. Without this principle, there can be no heaven and earth, no people, no thing, for they have nothing to contain them. It's only once principle exists that psychophysical stuff circulates everywhere, sending forth and nourishing the myriad things.

Is it principle that does the sending forth and the nourishing?

Zhu replied: Once principle exists this psychophysical stuff circulates everywhere, sending forth and nourishing things. Principle has no form or substance. (1.1, i.e., *juan* 1, page 1)

2. Under heaven there has never been psychophysical stuff without principle nor has there ever been principle without psychophysical stuff. (1.2)

3. Someone asked about principle and psychophysical stuff.

Zhu replied: Yichuan [Cheng Yi] explained it well, saying, "Principle is one, its manifestations are many."[3] When we speak of heaven, earth, and the myriad things together, there is but one principle. When it comes to people, each person has his or her own manifestation of the one principle. (1.2)

4. First there is heavenly principle, and then there is psychophysical stuff. Psychophysical stuff accumulates to become matter [*zhi* 質], and the nature of the thing [*xing*] is embedded within. (1.2)

5. Someone asked: Does principle exist first or psychophysical stuff?"

Zhu replied: Principle has never been separate from psychophysical stuff. But principle is "above form" and psychophysical stuff is "within form." From the point of view of what is above form and what is within form, can there possibly be no sequence?

Principle has no form, while psychophysical stuff is coarse and contains impurities. (1.3)

6. Someone asked: Is it the case that principle must exist first and only later will there be psychophysical stuff?

Zhu replied: Fundamentally, one can't speak of "first" and "later." But if we wish to trace back to their beginnings we would have to say that principle existed first. Still, principle is not a separate entity; it exists within this psychophysical stuff. If this psychophysical stuff did not exist, this principle would have nothing to adhere to. It is psychophysical stuff that makes for metal, wood, water, and fire; and principle that makes for goodness, righteousness, propriety, and wisdom. (1.3)

7. Someone asked: Does principle exist first and psychophysical stuff later?

Zhu replied: Fundamentally, principle and psychophysical stuff can't be spoken of in terms of "first" and "later." But, by inference, it would seem that principle exists first and psychophysical stuff later.

What evidence is there that principle exists in the psychophysical stuff?

Zhu replied: For instance, that there is order in the intermixing of the *yin* and *yang* and the five phases* is owing to principle. If psychophysical stuff didn't coalesce, principle would have nothing to adhere to. (1.3)

8. Someone asked about the statement that first there exists principle and later there exists psychophysical stuff.

Zhu replied: There is no need to speak like this. We know now that whether basically there first exists principle and then psychophysical stuff or psychophysical stuff and then principle can't be investigated. But if we were to speculate, I suspect

---

*Wuxing, the five phases or five activities, referring to wood, fire, earth, metal, and water.

psychophysical stuff depends on principle to operate. When this psychophysical stuff coalesces, principle too exists in it. It seems that psychophysical stuff is able to congeal and create and that principle, by contrast, does not feel, reckon, or create. It's just that wherever psychophysical stuff coalesces, principle exists within it. For instance, every person, plant, and animal born into this world has a seed; without a seed, it's not possible to produce a single thing. This is all a matter of psychophysical stuff. As for principle, it is just this pure, vast realm, with no physical existence. It cannot create anything. It is the psychophysical stuff that ferments and coalesces to produce things. But once the psychophysical stuff exists, principle exists within it. (1.3)

9. Someone asked: Do dry and withered things have principle or not?

Zhu replied: As soon as there exists a thing, there exists principle. Heaven has never produced a writing brush; people make brushes with rabbit hair. But as soon as there exists a brush, there exists principle. (4.61)

10. Someone asked: How do the "Way" and "principle" differ?

Zhu replied: The Way refers to a path, principle refers to a pattern.

Someone asked: Like the grain in wood?

Yes.

There was a further question: If this is the case, they would seem to be similar?

Zhu replied: The Way is all-embracing; principle refers to the many patterned veins within the way. And he added, the Way is vast, principle is detailed. (6.99)

11. Principle has its articulated manifestations. True goodness [*ren* 仁], righteousness [*yi* 義], propriety [*li* 禮], and wisdom [*zhi* 智] is each possessed of it. (6.99)

12. Someone asked: The ten thousand things are marvelous. But are they the same or not?

Zhu replied: Principle is but one. The principle of the Way is the same, but its manifestations are different. The relationship between a sovereign and minister has a principle for the relationship between a sovereign and minister; the relationship between a father and a son has a principle for the relationship between a father and a son. (6.99)

13. If principle has no affairs, it has nothing to attach to. (6.100)

B. HEAVEN AND EARTH

14. Someone asked: Is the mind-heart[†] of heaven and earth indeed spiritually efficacious (*ling*)? Or is it simply indifferent, taking no deliberate action [*wuwei* 無為]?

Zhu replied: You can't say that the mind-heart of heaven and earth is not spiritually efficacious, and yet it doesn't deliberate the way the human mind-heart does. Yichuan [Cheng Yi] said, "Heaven and earth has no mind-heart but creates; the sage has a mind-heart but acts without deliberation [*wuwei*]."[4] (1.4)

15. Someone asked: In the phrases "the mind-heart of heaven and earth" and "the principle of heaven and earth," principle refers to the principle of the Way. Does mind-heart have the meaning of "master?"

Zhu replied: Mind-heart does indeed have the meaning of "master," and what is meant by master is this principle. It isn't that principle exists separately from the mind-heart and that the mind-heart exists separately from principle. He further said, the

---

[†]In the Chinese tradition, *xin* 心 is both the source of people's intellect and understanding and the center of their emotions. Hence the translation "mind-heart."

word "person" [*ren* 人] is to heaven [*tian* 天], as the word "mind-heart" [*xin*] is to lord [*di* 帝]. (1.4)

16. Daofu[5] [Yang Daofu] said: Previously you instructed us to consider whether heaven and earth have a mind-heart or not. Lately, I've been thinking about it and I'd venture to say that heaven and earth have no mind-heart. True goodness is the mind-heart of heaven and earth. If they did have a mind-heart, it would necessarily ponder and plan. And why would heaven and earth ever have to ponder! That "the four seasons follow their course and the hundred things are born,"[6] I believe, is that they do just what they are supposed to do—no thought is needed. This is the Way of heaven and earth.

Zhu replied: If that's so, what do you make of the passages in the *Book of Changes*, "Do we not see in the *fu* 復 hexagram the mind-heart of heaven and earth"[7] and "Great and right: thus we can behold the feelings of heaven and earth?"[8] What you have said explains only their no mind-heart aspect. But if they had no mind-heart, cows would necessarily produce horses and peach trees would send forth plum blossoms—and other things too would happen of their own. Master Cheng said, "We refer to the controlling power [of heaven and earth] as *di* (lord) and the nature and feelings [of heaven and earth] as *qian* 乾."[9] These are established terms. The mind-heart is heaven and earth's controlling power; and so we say that the production of things is a matter of heaven and earth's mind-heart. Now Qinfu [Zhang Shi][10] thinks that I should not explain it like this. But I believe that heaven and earth have no appointed tasks and that the production of things is only a matter of their mind-heart. The primordial psychophysical stuff revolves and circulates freely, never stopping for even a moment. It just goes on generating the many, myriad things.

Someone asked: Didn't Master Cheng say, "Heaven and earth has no mind-heart but creates; the sage has a mind-heart but acts without deliberation [*wuwei*]"?[11]

Zhu replied: This speaks of the no-mind-heart aspect of heaven and earth. Consider the case of "the four seasons follow their course and the hundred things are born." In what way do heaven and earth employ a mind-heart? As for the sage, he accords with principle and that is all. What more deliberate action [*wei* 為] is there! Thus, Mingdao [Cheng Hao] explained it extremely well when he said, "The constancy of heaven and earth is that it extends the mind-heart to the ten thousand things, but without conscious deliberation; the constancy of the sage is that his emotions accord with the ten thousand affairs but without personal feelings."

Someone asked: Isn't it that the mind-heart extends to the ten thousand things, but everywhere is without self-interest [*wusi* 無私]?

Zhu replied: Heaven and earth extend this mind-heart to the myriad things. When man receives it, it thereupon becomes the mind-heart of man; when things receive it, it thereupon becomes the mind-heart of things; when plants and animals get it, it becomes the mind-heart of plants and animals—it is just the one mind-heart of heaven and earth. Now, it is essential that we understand the mind-heart aspect of heaven and earth. Essential too that we apprehend heaven and earth's no mind-heart aspect. It does not lend itself to a definitive explanation. (1.4)

17. The azure sky is called heaven. It revolves round and round and flows everywhere, never stopping. And when nowadays it's said that there's a person in heaven judging our wrongdoings, that definitely can't be. Neither can it be said that the Way has no master at all! This is something people need to understand. (1.5)

18. In the beginning, heaven and earth were simply yin and yang psychophysical stuff. This psychophysical stuff circulated, spinning around and round; spinning furiously, the coarse

sediment became compressed, and, because there was no place for it to escape, it congealed into solid earth at the center. The refined psychophysical stuff became heaven, the sun, the moon, and the heavenly bodies. They are on the outside only, constantly revolving round and round; earth is at the center, unmoving. It is not that earth is underneath. (1.6)

19. The pure and robust stuff became heaven; the heavy and turbid stuff became earth. (1.6)

20. The heavens revolve without stop, turning day and night. It's for this reason that earth is compressed in the center. If the heavens stopped for even a moment, earth would be sure to fall out. It is merely because of the furious revolution of the heavens that the abundant sediment congeals in the middle. Earth is the coarse sediment of the psychophysical stuff. It is for this reason that it is said [in the *Huainanzi* 淮南子] "the light and pure are heaven, the heavy and turbid are earth." (1.6)

21. With its psychophysical stuff heaven leans on earth's physical form; with its physical form earth attaches itself to heaven's psychophysical stuff. Heaven embodies earth. Earth is the one especially prominent thing within heaven. Heaven's psychophysical stuff revolves on the outside, and as a consequence earth is compressed in the center, collapsed and with no movement. If the heavens were to stop for even a moment, earth would be sure to fall out. (1.6)

22. In the beginning, when heaven and earth were an undifferentiated chaos, I think only water and fire, these two phases, existed. Sediment in the water formed the earth. Today, when we climb up to some high spot and look around, the mountains are all in the shape of waves—this is how the water drifted. We just don't know when the sediment congealed. Initially, it was extremely soft and only later, when it congealed, did it harden.

Someone asked: I guess this is like the tides making sand into mounds?

Zhu replied: Yes, it is. The most turbid water became earth and the purest fire became things like the wind, the thunder, the lightning, the sun, and the stars. (1.7)

23. There exist the far reaches of the earth. Emperor Taizong [r. 626–649] of the Tang attacked the Guligan [a minority people in the Gobi Desert] and established a military governorship at Jiankun. This place tended to remain bright at night. The night did not get very dark because the place was at the far reaches of the earth and the sun's light shone directly on it [since the sun was at the edge nearby]. Everybody's hair there was the color of fire. (1.7)

24. Someone asked: Kangjie[12] [Shao Yong 邵雍] talked about what is "beyond the six points of the universe" [north, south, east, west, zenith, and nadir], but there is no "beyond," is there?

Zhu replied: With respect to principle there is no "within" and "beyond," but with respect to the arrangement of the six points of the universe there most definitely is a "within" and "beyond." The sun arises along the eastern edge and sinks along the western edge. The next day it once again arises along the eastern edge. There is a great deal above and a great deal below as well. Is it not then "within the six points!" In calculating psychophysical stuff, astronomers simply calculate the orbital movement of the sun, moon, and heavenly bodies. They can't calculate what is above, but can it be there is no "within" and "beyond!" (1.7)

25. Someone asked: Not ten thousand years have passed since the very beginning. What was it like before that?

Zhu said: It's clear that it must have been like this before as well.

Someone further asked: Are heaven and earth able to fall into ruin?

Zhu said: They are unable to fall into ruin. But when Waylessness among people becomes extreme, everything becomes enveloped together in a kind of chaos and people and things are all extinguished. And then they are born again new.

Someone asked: How was it that the first people were born?

Zhu said: They were transformed out of psychophysical stuff. The essence of the two [yin and yang] and the five [phases] came together and took on form. The Buddhists call this *huasheng* 化生, "birth by transformation." For them, the number of things "born by transformation" nowadays is very considerable—even lice, for example. (1.7)

26. The process of creation is like a grinding mill. The upper part goes around and round without stop. The myriad things that come into being are like the milled grounds. Some are coarse, some are refined—they're naturally not uniform. (1.8)

27. Keji asked: "The great potter fashions all creatures."[13] Once they are gone are they gone for good or is there a principle for their going and then returning?

Zhu said: Once they are gone, they are simply gone for good. How can there be psychophysical stuff that disperses and then re-coalesces? (1.8)

28. Yin and yang are psychophysical stuff. The five phases are matter [*zhi*].[14] From this matter, things are produced. Although the five phases are matter, it is only because they also possess the psychophysical stuff of the five phases that things are produced from them. It's that the yin and yang psychophysical stuff[15] divide into five. It is not that beyond yin and yang the five phases separately exist. (1.9)

29. The five phases are made up of both yin and yang and each one of the five itself is made up of yin and yang. (1.9)

30. The most refined part of psychophysical stuff is the *shen* 神 expansive spirit.[16] Metal, wood, water, fire, and earth [the five phases] are not *shen* expansive spirit, but they become metal, wood, water, fire, and earth because of the *shen* expansive spirit.

In human beings, it [the most refined part] is principle; we become
benevolent, righteous, proprietary, wise, and trustworthy because
of principle. (1.9)

31. Water and fire are pure; metal and wood are turbid; earth
is turbid as well. (1.10)

32. Heaven has spring, summer, fall, and winter; earth has
metal, wood, water, and fire; and people have goodness, righteousness, propriety, and wisdom. In each, the four things operate mutually. (1.11)

33. Heaven makes a full rotation around the earth in one
day—and then goes an additional degree. The sun reaches this
same spot, one full rotation, but cannot make up the additional
degree. The moon lags behind by 13 degrees. When heaven's
extra degree per day totals 365 and ¼ degrees, it catches up to
the sun. And, as in the case of the sun, it will have been one year.
(2.13)

34. The moon is always round and never wanes. It is just that
it constantly receives sunlight to become bright. On the third or
fourth day, the sun illumines it from below so when people here
look at it, they see just a crescent of light. And on the fifteenth
or sixteenth day, when the sun is below the earth and its light
shoots out from the earth's four sides, the moon is brightened by
that light, with earth's shadow in the middle. The ancients and
our contemporaries alike say that the moon is waning. Only Shen
Cunzhong[17] said there is no waning. (2.19)

35. The eclipse of the sun is a matter of its being blocked by
the moon, and the eclipse of the moon is a matter of its contend-
ing with the sun. Once the moon backs off from the sun a little,
then the eclipse ceases. (2.21)

36. Someone asked about the belief that the dragon produces
rain.

Zhu replied: The dragon is an aquatic creature. It rises up and,
as it mingles with the yang psychophysical stuff, it steams, and

so is able to produce rain. But conventional rain is produced naturally by the vapors arising from the yin and yang psychophysical stuff and is not necessarily the doings of a dragon. [The *Book of Changes* says,] "Thick clouds, no rain—they keep moving away"[18]: here it seems just that the psychophysical stuff from below ascends ever higher and so it can't rain. Only when the psychophysical stuff provides cover and does not disperse can there be rain. In discussing wind, thunder, clouds and rain, Zhang Zai's *Correcting Youthful Ignorance* [*Zhengmeng* 正蒙] is exceedingly clear. (2.23)

C. Spirit Beings

37. Someone asked: Do spirits exist or not?

Zhu said: How can I quickly explain the matter to you? And if I did, would you possibly believe me? You must gradually come to understand the multitudinous manifestations of principle, and then these doubts of yours will resolve on their own. [In the *Analects* we read] "Fan Chi asked about wisdom. The Master said: 'To give one's self earnestly to the duties due to people, and, while respecting spirits, to keep them at a distance, may be called wisdom.'"[19] Let people grasp matters that should be grasped and put aside those that can't. When the ordinary matters of daily life have been fully grasped, the principle of spirit beings will naturally become clear—this then constitutes wisdom. This is precisely what is meant [by the Master's remark], "Unable able to serve humanity, how can we serve *gui* spirits?"[20] (3.33)

38. The matter of spirits is naturally a secondary one. They have neither form nor shadow; this is difficult to grasp, but there is no need to. Better to expend your efforts on the urgent matters of daily life. "Unable to serve humanity, how can we serve *gui* spirits? Not understanding life, how can we understand death?"[21] (3.33)

39. Rain and wind, dew and lightning, sun and moon, day and night, these are all traces of spirits; these are the just and upright spirits of broad daylight. As for those who are said to "howl from the rafters and butt people in the chest," these we call the unjust and depraved spirits; they sometimes exist and sometimes do not, sometimes go and sometimes come, sometimes coalesce and sometimes disperse. In addition, there is the saying "pray to them and they will respond, pray to them and they will grant fulfillment;" these too are what we call spirits. These are all of one and the same principle. The myriad affairs of the world are all of this principle—among them there's merely a difference in degree of refinement and size. (3.34)

EXPANSIVE AND CONTRACTIVE FORCES OF NATURE

40. The *shen* spirit expands; the *gui* spirit contracts. For instance, when wind, rain, thunder, and lightning first issue forth, this is the operation of the *shen* expansive spirit; as the wind dies, the rain passes, the thunder stops, and the lightning ceases, this is the operation of the *gui* contractive spirit. (3.34)

41. The *gui* contractive spirit and the *shen* expansive spirit are nothing more than the waxing and waning of the yin and yang. The transforming and nourishing operations of nature and the darkening of the sky that ensues with wind and rain are all owing to these spirits. In human beings, the vital spirit [*jing* 精] is the earthly soul [*po* 魄] and the earthly soul is the *gui* contractive spirit in abundance; the psychophysical stuff is the heavenly soul [*hun* 魂], and the heavenly soul is the *shen* expansive spirit in abundance.[22] [As the *Book of Changes* says]: "The vital spirit [*jing*] and psychophysical stuff coalesce to constitute a thing." What thing then is without the *gui* and *shen* spirits? [As the *Book of Changes* continues:] "The floating up of the heavenly soul constitutes a fluxion."[23] When the heavenly soul floats up, we can be sure of the earthly soul's descent. (3.34)

42. The *guishen* spirits are simply psychophysical stuff. What contracts and expands, comes and goes, is psychophysical stuff. In heaven and earth there is nothing that is not psychophysical stuff. The psychophysical stuff of human beings and that of heaven and earth are everywhere interconnected. People themselves don't realize this. As soon as the human mind-heart becomes active, it is bound to affect psychophysical stuff; the mind-heart and psychophysical stuff—in its contractions and expansions, its comings and goings—mutually influence each other. Consider divination. Whenever you divine, you're giving expressing to what's in your mind-heart; with such activation, there's certain to be a response. (3.34)

43. Someone asked: Are spirits simply this psychophysical stuff or not?

Zhu said: They are like the spiritual efficaciousness within this psychophysical stuff. (3.34)

GHOSTS, SPIRITS, AND MONSTERS

44. They were talking about how Xie Shilong's household had seen a ghost [*gui*] and Zhu said: In the world those who believe in spirits all say that they really do exist between heaven and earth. Those who do not believe in them absolutely think there are no ghosts. And yet there are those who have truly seen them. Zheng Jingwang consequently believed that what the Xies had seen was real, and that they simply didn't understand that it was just a special type of rainbow.

Bida then asked: Is a rainbow simply psychophysical stuff or does it have substance?

Zhu said: Since it is able to sip water, it must have a stomach; only when it disperses does it become nonexistent. It's like thunder and spirits—these are similar things. (3.36)

45. They were speaking of ghosts (*gui*) and monsters [*guai* 怪] and Zhu said: The spirits of wood are the one-footed *kui* 夔 and

the *wangliang* 魍魎. The *kui* has only one foot. In antiquity there was talk of *wangliang*. If ghosts and monsters really do exist, they must be creatures such as these. (3.36)

46. Someone asked about the principle of life and death and of spirits.

Zhu said: The Way of heaven flows everywhere, nourishing the ten thousand things. There is principle and only afterward is there psychophysical stuff. They exist simultaneously, yet in the end principle is thought to be the master. Human beings receive them and possess life. The clear part of the psychophysical stuff becomes psychophysical stuff, the turbid part becomes solid matter [*zhi*].[24] Consciousness and activity are the work of the yang [psychophysical stuff] while the body with its form and shape is the work of the yin [psychophysical stuff]. Psychophysical stuff is called the heavenly soul; the body is called the earthly soul. The *Huainanzi* commentary by Gao You says: "The heavenly soul is the yang's *shen* spirit; the earthly soul is the yin's *shen* spirit."[25] What we call the *shen* spirit then is master of the bodily psychophysical stuff. A person is born because essence (*jing*) and psychophysical stuff coalesce; but a person only has so much psychophysical stuff, which in time necessarily is exhausted. When it is exhausted, the psychophysical stuff of the heavenly soul returns to heaven and the bodily form of the earthly soul returns to earth, and the person dies. When a person is about to die, the warm psychophysical stuff rises; this is what is called the "heavenly soul ascending." The lower half of the body gradually cools; this is called the "earthly soul descending." Thus, if there is life, there must be death; if there is a beginning, there must be an end. What coalesces and disperses is the psychophysical stuff. As for principle, it is simply lodged in the psychophysical stuff —it's not something that at the outset congeals to become a distinct thing by itself. Merely whatever is appropriate for a human being to do is principle; principle can't be spoken of as coalescing or dispersing.

Now when a person dies, though in the end he returns to a state of dispersal, he does not disperse completely at once. Thus, in religious sacrifice there is the principle of influence and response. In the case of a distant ancestor we can't know whether his psychophysical stuff exists or not, yet because those offering sacrifices to him are his descendants they necessarily are of the same psychophysical stuff; and so there exists a principle of mutual influence and penetration. Still, psychophysical stuff that is already dispersed does not coalesce again. The Buddhists, however, think that a person at death becomes a *gui* spirit and that the *gui* spirit returns as a person. If this were so, then between heaven and earth there would always be the same number of people coming and going and still less would people be produced and reproduced by the creative process. This is absolutely absurd. As to Boyou's becoming an evil spirit,[‡] Yichuan [Cheng Yi] said that it was of a special kind of principle of the Way.[26] It would seem that before his psychophysical stuff had been fully exhausted, he met a violent death and so naturally was able to become an evil spirit. Zichan[27] appointed someone to serve as his heir so that his spirit would have a place to go and hence would not become an evil spirit. It can indeed be said that Zichan "understood the circumstances of spirit beings."[28]

Someone asked: Yichuan said that "*guishen* spirits are traces of the creative process."[29] Is it possible that these are indeed traces of the creative process?

Zhu said: They are. To speak of the standard principle, it is like a tree suddenly producing blossoms and leaves—these are traces of the creative process. It is also like lightning, thunder, wind, or rain suddenly filling the air. These are traces too. It's

---

[‡]The *Zuo Commentary*, 551, 557, and 618, tells of how Boyou from the state of Zheng was killed in the sheep market by Zishi and his men-at-arms, and how years later he appeared as a ghost to wreak vengeance.

just that they are what people ordinarily see and so they don't think them strange. When suddenly they hear a *gui* ghost howling or see a *gui* ghost in flames, these they consider strange. They do not appreciate that these, too, are traces of the creative process. It is just because they are not of the standard principle that people regard them as strange. For instance, the *School Sayings of Confucius* [*Kongzi jiayu* 孔子家語] says: "The monsters of the mountains are called *kui* [the one-footed monster] and *wangliang*, the monsters of the water are called *long* 龍 [dragons] and *wang-xiang*, and the monsters of the earth are called *fenyang* 羵羊."[30] All these are produced by confused and perverse psychophysical stuff and are surely not without principle—you mustn't insist that they are without principle. It is like the winter's being cold and the summer's being warm; this is the standard principle. But there are times when suddenly it turns cold in the summer or warm in the winter. Can we possibly say there is not a principle for this! Still, because it is not an ordinary principle, we consider it strange. Confucius consequently did not speak of such matters; and, likewise, there is no need for students to pay them any heed. (3.36)

47. Yongzhi said: As human beings, in praying to heaven, earth, mountains, and rivers, we rely on what we possess to influence what they possess [i.e., psychophysical stuff]. As descendants sacrificing to ancestors, we rely on what we possess to influence what they don't.

Zhu replied: The psychophysical stuff of the spirits of heaven and earth is constantly contracting and expanding without stop. The psychophysical stuff of a person's *gui* spirit dissipates until there is nothing left. This dissipation can take more time or less time. There are people who do not readily submit to death and, as a consequence, when they die their psychophysical stuff does not disperse, and they become evil beings [*yao* 妖] and monsters. In the case of a person who has met a cruel death, or a Buddhist or Daoist who dies, oftentimes the psychophysical stuff will not disperse. As for sages and worthies, they are at ease in their deaths, so how could their psychophysical stuff possibly not disperse—how could they become spirits or monsters? Take Huangdi, Yao, and Shun: no one has ever heard that they died and became spirits or monsters. (3.39)

48. Someone asked: What about those people who die but whose psychophysical stuff doesn't disperse?

Zhu said: They are ones who do not readily submit to death. Take, for instance, those who bring punishment or harm to themselves: they don't easily submit to death and, still more, keep their vital spirit [*jingshen* 精神] concentrated. Those accepting of their deaths naturally have no psychophysical stuff left. How could one ever believe that Yao or Shun became a *gui* ghost? (3.43)

49. For the psychophysical stuff to disperse at death— extinguished without trace—is the norm. Such is the principle of the Way. As for returning to life, this is a matter of the coalesced psychophysical stuff unexpectedly not dispersing. How, after all, can one intentionally keep one's living psychophysical stuff concentrated so as to be born a second time? It's not the norm. Yichuan [Cheng Yi] said: "In the *Zuo Commentary* Boyou's becoming an evil spirit is of a special kind of principle." This is to say that it is not the normal principle of life and death. (3.44)

50. Guangzu was inquiring about the Master's letter in response to Songqing: What do you think of [Cheng Yi's comment], "Boyou's becoming an evil spirit is of a special kind of principle."

Zhu replied: It's natural there is such a principle. In most cases, it's that a person doesn't meet a natural death and, as a result, his strong psychophysical stuff doesn't disperse; yet with time, even it can't but disperse. For instance, in Zhangzhou there was a scandal involving a wife who killed her husband and secretly buried

him. Afterward he became an evil spirit; only when the matter
was exposed, did he cease being an evil spirit. Fearing that in this
matter officials would memorialize the throne to spare the wife's
life [and that the evil spirit would thus reappear], the people of
Zhangzhou sent a petition [calling for the punishment of the cul-
prits] to the various officials for their endorsement. Afterward
the wife was beheaded and her lover was hanged. Hence we know
from this case the general principle, that if we do not render a
conviction and give a life for a life, then the injustice suffered by
the dead one will not be undone. (3.44)

51. Someone asked: What about [Cheng Yi's remark that]
"the Boyou affair is of a special kind of principle?"

Zhu said: It is of a special kind of principle. The reason people get sick and come to their end is that their psychophysical
stuff disperses. But there are those people who meet with punishment as well as those who die quite suddenly. Their psychophysical stuff remains collected and does not disperse at first,
though in the end it, too, disperses completely. It's the same for
Buddhists and Daoists, who because they are obsessed with
their bodies and at death cannot hold on to them, in the end are
unhappy; in dying they harbor feelings of anger and, consequently, their psychophysical stuff does not disperse. (3.44)

52. Someone asked: [The *Book of Changes* says], "The floating
up of the heavenly soul constitutes a fluxion." Sometimes, it
becomes a monster. Why does it not disperse?

Zhu said: What is meant by the character *you* 遊, "floating
up," is very gradually to disperse. If it has become a monster,
in most cases it's because it didn't die a natural death and its
psychophysical stuff didn't disperse, and, as a result, it became
melancholy and transformed into a monster. In the case of a
person who's frail and dies from disease, his psychophysical
stuff becomes completely exhausted and he dies. How can he
possibly again turn melancholy and become a monster! Even

those who do not die a natural death will disperse with time. It's as if we were kneading dough and making paste today and, in the process a small clump formed of itself and didn't disperse; in time gradually it too would disperse on its own. It's like the case of Boyou. He, too, died without dispersing. Hengqu [Zhang Zai] said: "When a thing first comes into existence, the psychophysical stuff day by day infuses and nourishes it. As the thing matures and comes to its end, the psychophysical stuff day by day returns and then, floating up, disperses. The infusing is considered the *shen* spirit—because the psychophysical stuff is expanding. The contraction is considered the *gui* spirit—because the psychophysical stuff is returning."[31] The myriad things and affairs under heaven, from antiquity down to the present, are all simply the yin and yang waxing and waning, contracting and expanding. Hengqu, with his notions of contraction and expansion, explained it all extremely coherently. (3.45)

53. Someone inquired: Nowadays households frequently experience freak occurrences.

Zhu said: These are the doings of the demons of mountains and streams. In Jianzhou there was a scholar who in his travels met up with a one-footed man who asked the whereabouts of a certain household. The scholar accompanied him and saw him enter the household in question. A few days later that family, in fact, experienced the death of a son. (3.45)

54. There was discussion about shamans controlling *gui* ghosts and how *gui* ghosts mimic what the shamans do in order to resist them.

Zhu said: When the mind-hearts of the descendants are extremely crafty, they stimulate crafty psychophysical stuff and produce *gui* ghosts that are likewise cunning. (3.45)

55. Houzhi asked: There's probably no principle for a person's dying and becoming a wild animal. And yet, personally I have

seen a son in a Yongchun family who had ears of hog bristles and hog skin. What do you make of this?

Zhu said: This isn't supernatural. I've heard that a soldier employed in Jixi had hog bristles on his chest and when asleep made hog noises. This is simply because he had been endowed with the psychophysical stuff of a hog. (3.46)

56. Someone asked: In sacrificing animals, offerings, and libations to heaven, earth, mountains, and rivers are we just expressing our authentic mind-heart, or is there truly psychophysical stuff that comes in response?

Zhu said: If we say that nothing comes to accept the sacrificial offerings, what are we sacrificing to? Yet what sort of thing is so majestic above that people worship and reverence it? It would be absurd to say that a cloud-chariot actually comes in response. (3.51)

57. Someone asked: In the world there are *shen* spirits who for hundreds of years running have received temple sacrifices. What is the principle for this?

Zhu said: Gradually, after a while, even those spirits are able to disperse. Formerly, when I was serving as prefect in Nankang, because of a sustained drought people everywhere were praying to *shen* spirits. I happened upon a certain temple, which had just three ramshackle buildings in utter ruin. The person there said that thirty to fifty years ago the efficacy of [that temple's] spirit was quick as an echo and so people would come visit and the spirit would speak to them from behind a hanging screen. Such was the power of the spirit's efficacy (*ling*) in the past; nowadays this spirit's efficacy is like this. You can see for yourselves. (3.53).

58. It's customary these days to honor *gui* ghosts. To be in Xin'an [in Anhui] and other places is like being in a den of *gui* ghosts morning and night. One time I returned to my native village [in Wuyuan county]. The so-called Five Transmitters Temple is located there. It is most wondrous and mysterious and

embraced by all, who believe that fortune and misfortune make themselves known right there on the spot. When locals are about to travel away from home, they take slips of paper [in the shape of money, houses, animals, etc.] to the temple, offer prayers, and only afterward begin their journey. And scholars passing through the area present their name cards and announce, "Disciple So-and-So is paying a visit to the temple." When I first returned, kinsmen urgently bid me to go, but I didn't. That night they assembled the clan members together for a banquet. They had gone to the government office to buy wine, which was contaminated with ashes. As soon as I drank it, I came down with a severe stomachache that lasted through the night. On top of that, the next day, by chance, there appeared a snake at the side of the stairs. Everyone was in a great uproar and thought that it was because I hadn't paid a visit to the temple. I told them: "I got sick because my stomach didn't digest the food. It has nothing to do with the temple. Do not blame the spirit of the Five Transmitters." There was a certain man in the family, one with some learning, and he too came to encourage me to go to the temple, saying "this is the common practice." I told him, "Why should it be a common practice? It's surprising that even you would speak this way. Having had the good fortune of returning home, I am very near my ancestral graves. If the spirit is capable of causing fortune and misfortune, please kindly bury me at the side of the ancestral graves—it would be most convenient."

Zhu further said: In serving as local officials, we must get rid of cults to licentious deities. If though, it's one with an imperial plaque, we can't lightly rid ourselves of them. (3.53).

59. They were talking about an affair in which the Purple Maiden goddess[32] had been invited to recite verse. Zhu said: When she was invited to appear in person, a little girl from the family appeared. We don't know what to make of this. Just as in Quzhou, a man who served a certain spirit merely recorded a list

of inquiries on a piece of paper and sealed it in front of the spirit's temple. A little later, he opened up the sealed list, and on the paper, spontaneously, were the answers to the inquiries. We don't know how this could be. (3.54)

60. Someone asked: I have tried asking before about the Purple Maiden Goddess.

Zhu said: Because it [i.e., the response] is in our own mind-heart, she's able to respond; when she's unable to respond it's because our mind-heart doesn't quite understand the complexity of the matter. (3.55)

61. Someone asked: As for principle of the Way, there are upright manifestations and there are depraved ones, there are right ones and there are wrong ones. This is the case, too, with spirits. In the world there are perverse spirits; it can't be said that no such principle exists.

Zhu said: Laozi remarked [*Laozi*, chap. 60], "When the empire is ruled in accordance with the Way, the *gui* spirits lose their numinous powers." If the kingly way were cultivated and illumined, this sort of perverse psychophysical stuff would completely dissolve. (3.55)

ANCESTRAL SPIRITS

62. Someone inquired: Human nature is principle, which can't be spoken of as coalescing and dispersing. What coalesces to be born and disperses to die is psychophysical stuff and nothing more. The so-called vital spirit, the heavenly and earthly souls, and perception and consciousness are psychophysical stuff. Consequently, when it coalesces there's existence, and when it disperses there's nonexistence. As for principle, it has always existed, from antiquity to the present. It does not repeatedly coalesce and disperse or wax and wane.

Zhu replied: It's simply that this yin and yang psychophysical stuff of heaven and earth is received by human beings and the myriad things. The psychophysical stuff coalesces and becomes a person, disperses and becomes a *gui* contractive spirit. But even though this psychophysical stuff has dispersed, this principle of heaven and earth and yin and yang produces and reproduces endlessly. And while the vital spirit and the heavenly and earthly souls of the ancestors may have already dispersed, the vital spirit and the heavenly and earthly souls of the descendants naturally have some affinity with them. As a consequence, if in performing rituals of sacrifice the descendants are authentic [*cheng* 誠] and reverentially attentive [*jing* 敬],[33] they can make contact with the heavenly and earthly souls of the ancestors. Naturally this is difficult to talk about. If you look for them once they have dispersed, it seems as if they have no existence whatsoever, and yet if you're able to be authentic and reverentially attentive there will be influence and response. This too is because the principle for it has always simply existed right here [perhaps pointing to his body]. (3.46)

63. From the point of view of heaven and earth, there is just one psychophysical stuff. From the point of view of one body, my psychophysical stuff is the psychophysical stuff of my ancestors—it's just one and the same psychophysical stuff. So, just as soon as there is influence there is bound to be a response. (3.47)

64. Chen Houzhi asked: The ancestors are a collective of psychophysical stuff between heaven and earth. And when descendants sacrifice to them, they coalesce and then they disperse.

Zhu replied: This then is what Shangcai [Xie Liangzuo] meant in commenting "When you want them to exist, they exist; when you want them to be nonexistent, they're nonexistent.'[34] It's all due to human beings. Spirits are things with a fundamental existence; ancestors too are of this same psychophysical stuff, but they possess a guiding intelligence. When the descendants are present bodily here, the psychophysical stuff of the ancestors then becomes present here. The same blood and pulse runs through them all. The reason *"shen* spirits do not enjoy the offerings of those not of their kindred and people do not sacrifice to those not of their ancestry" [as the *Zuo Commentary* states][35] is simply that their psychophysical stuff is unrelated. As for the Son of Heaven sacrificing to heaven and earth, the various lords sacrificing to the mountains and rivers, and the great officers sacrificing to the five deities [being the spirits of the outer door, the inner door, the walk, the hearth, and the center of the room]: though they [meaning heaven and earth, the mountains and rivers, and the five deities] are not these men's ancestors, the Son of Heaven is still master of all under heaven, the various lords are masters of the mountains and rivers, and the great officers are masters of the five deities. And because they are masters over them, the psychophysical stuff [of heaven and earth, the mountains and rivers, and the five deities] also presides in their bodies. This being so, there is an affinity between them. (3.47)

65. Someone inquired: When a person dies, I don't know whether the heavenly *hun* and earthly *po* souls disperse or not.

Zhu said: They do indeed disperse.

Someone further inquired: How about the descendants' wherewithal to influence them through sacrifice?

Zhu said: In the end, the descendants are of the same psychophysical stuff as the ancestors, so even though the ancestors' psychophysical stuff may have dispersed, their blood line [literally, roots] still exists right here. If we're wholeheartedly authentic and reverentially attentive, we, in fact, are able to summon their psychophysical stuff so that it coalesces right here. It's the same as water and waves: the water that comes later is not the earlier water, the waves that come later are not the earlier waves, and yet all of it is just the same water and waves. The relationship between the psychophysical stuff of the descendants and the psychophysical stuff of the ancestors is just like this. The ancestors' psychophysical stuff may promptly disperse of itself, yet their blood line nonetheless exists right here. And since their blood line exists here, the fact is we're able to induce their psychophysical stuff into coalescing right here. This matter is difficult to talk about so I just ask that you consider it for yourselves. (3.47)

66. We can speak of the spirits as controlling powers, but we can't speak of them as things [*wu* 物]. And they are not like the clay-modeled spirits we find nowadays. They are simply psychophysical stuff. Suppose you are sacrificing to them; you just have to concentrate your vital spirit if you're going to influence them. Ancestors are of the same psychophysical stuff you've inherited, and thus you can influence them. (3.49)

67. The "influence and response" [gange 感格] that takes place during sacrificial offerings sometimes happens in the yin [psychophysical stuff] and sometimes in the yang [psychophysical stuff]. Since everything follows its own kind, when attracted the ancestor simply comes. It isn't that there's a thing amassed in the void out there waiting for descendants to seek it. It's just that in making the offering, when the sacrificer "influences" the ancestral spirit with complete authenticity and reverential attentiveness, the spirit's psychophysical stuff is sure to lodge itself right here. (3.50)

68. Someone asked about the principle of sacrificing: Is it a matter [as Fan Zuyu said] that "with authenticity the *shen* spirit comes into existence, and without authenticity the *shen* spirit has no existence?"[36]

Zhu replied, The principle of *guishen* spirits is the principle in our mind-heart. (3.50)

69. Someone asked: In offering sacrifices, the descendant makes his intentions fully true in order to get the vital spirit of his ancestor to coalesce. I don't know, though, whether this is a matter of bringing about a union of the ancestor's heavenly and

earthly souls or simply of influencing the psychophysical stuff of his heavenly soul.

Zhu said: To burn "southernwood and offer it with fat" [as recounted in the *Book of Poetry*] is for the purpose of repaying the ancestor's psychophysical stuff. "To offer libations of fragrant spirits" [as the *Book of Rites* suggests] is for the purpose of summoning home the heavenly soul, that is, to bring it together with the earthly soul. And, as it says [in the *Book of Rites*]: "It is the union of the *gui* and *shen* spirits that constitutes our doctrine in perfection."

Someone further asked: I don't know whether it's always like this or like this only at the time of sacrificial offerings.

Zhu said: It's only if the psychophysical stuff of the descendant is present that the ancestor's psychophysical stuff is present. When there are no sacrificial offerings, how can the ancestor's psychophysical stuff coalesce? (3.50)

70. Someone asked: Once an ancestor's vital spirit departs, a person must "fast for seven days and hold vigil for three days," "seeking it in the yang and seeking it in the yin" [as prescribed by the *Book of Rites*], and only then will he get it to coalesce. This being the case, when it coalesces, it does so suddenly. And as soon as the praying and sacrificing have come to an end and his authenticity and reverential attentiveness have dispersed, it too suddenly disperses.

Zhu replied: That's right. (3.50)

71. Someone asked: When a person dies and the psychophysical stuff of his heavenly soul disperses, we set up a master [of ceremonies] to serve as master over it. It's essential that he bring together some of the psychophysical stuff right here, isn't it?

Zhu said: When a death first occurred, the ancients would summon the heavenly soul to return to the earthly soul, set up a double, and establish a master. This is because they always hoped to connect with some of the dead person's vital spirit right here. In the ancient practice of consecrating the tortoise shell [for divination] they used the blood of a sacrificial animal, and they did so because they believed that that tortoise shell after a while no longer possessed spiritual power and so used some living psychophysical stuff to connect with [the spirits]. In the "Monograph on Divining" in the *Records of the Grand Historian* (*Shiji* 史記), to foretell the events of spring they rubbed the tortoise shell with a hen's egg and divined; this was to take living psychophysical stuff to connect with [the spirits] and is the meaning of consecrating the tortoise shell. He added: The ancients set up the impersonator of the dead. This too was to take the living psychophysical stuff of a live person to connect with [the spirit of the dead]. (3.50)

Like everything else in the universe, human beings are constituted of principle and psychophysical stuff. The principle for
being human is the same in each and every person. Following
Cheng Yi, Zhu Xi identifies this principle in human beings as
the originally good nature composed of the cardinal virtues—
true goodness, righteousness, propriety, and wisdom—first
described by Mencius in the fourth century BCE.

But, as Zhang Zai before him maintained, Zhu insists that
each of us at birth also receives an endowment of psychophysical
stuff, the quality and quantity of which differs. It is the particular quality and quantity of this psychophysical stuff that gives
each of us our particular characteristics and distinguishes one
person from another. Some of us will get stuff that is refined and
clear, some will get stuff that is turbid and dark, some stuff will
be balanced, and some will be one-sided. Differences in the
endowments give rise to differences in people. In short, psychophysical stuff accounts for individuation in human beings.

The question of why this person gets this particular allotment
of psychophysical stuff and that person gets that allotment of psychophysical stuff has a simple answer: it is random. When a person is born, the ever-circulating psychophysical stuff of the

universe spins off a share to constitute that person. Principle and psychophysical stuff converge to produce that person. And the quantity and quality of that share accounts for the psychophysical attributes of that person. (4.65)

Thus, building on the ideas of his Northern Song predecessors, Zhu provides a coherent answer to a question left largely unanswered by Mencius, namely: If all people are born inherently good, why is it that some manifest that goodness and others do not? Psychophysical stuff is the key. An endowment that is turbid, coarse, or one-sided can effectively obscure principle, making it impossible for the good human nature to become manifest. Henceforth, the Confucian tradition could embrace Mencius's appealing notion of the goodness of human nature while still explaining the presence of evil in humankind. It is important to underscore here that Zhu never characterizes psychophysical stuff itself as "evil" or "bad." Certain characteristics of one's endowment of psychophysical stuff (excessive turbidity or density, for example) may prevent one from accessing the inherent goodness within and may result in that person becoming evil or bad. But the stuff itself is not evil or bad.

For clarity's sake, Zhu Xi speaks of two distinct natures in human beings. There is the original nature, which—comprising true goodness, righteousness, propriety, and wisdom—is identical in all of us. This nature is one with principle. Then there is what he calls the psychophysical nature, which refers to the original nature combined with our psychophysical endowment. The psychophysical natures in human beings, of course, are different.

Humankind thus faces a dilemma: each person is born with an innate goodness; but a person's own psychophysical limitations can make it challenging to access that goodness. This dilemma, though, is by no means insurmountable—and this point is essential for understanding Zhu's philosophical program.

For the psychophysical stuff is malleable, and can be molded and reshaped, and sufficiently refined so that the good nature that inheres is no longer obscured or covered by it. This, no doubt, takes effort and commitment. And this is where Zhu's elaborate self-cultivation process, laid out in the next few chapters, comes in.

Zhu devotes considerable attention to the role that the mind-heart must play in the effort to nurture and refine the psychophysical stuff. He says that it is precisely the mind-heart that enables people to recognize the limitations imposed by their psychophysical endowments, address those limitations, and thereby realize the innate goodness of their original human nature. But the mind-heart does not necessarily cooperate. Following Zhang Zai,[1] he explains that the mind-heart "is the master of the nature and the emotions" (5.89), thus understanding that the duty of the mind-heart is to keep at bay not only human emotions but also, especially, the selfish desires that excessive emotions can generate. By maintaining control over emotions and desires, the mind-heart prevents them from inundating the good nature and covering it over. If the mind-heart fails here, a person loses access to the innate goodness and is sure to lose the Way. Zhu admonishes: "Clear out all selfish desires and heavenly principle will flow forth. This is to be truly good." And, he suggests, the role of *zhi* 志, one's will or sense of purpose, is to set the mind-heart in the right direction.

A. Human Nature and the Nature of Things

1. Someone asked: The nature of human beings and things has one source, so how is it that there are differences among them?

Zhu replied: We speak of human nature as bright or dim; the nature of things is simply one-sided and blocked. Dim natures can be made bright. But already one-sided and blocked natures cannot be penetrated. Hengqu [Zhang Zai] said, "Everything in the world has its nature. Whether it is penetrable or covered, open or blocked, is what accounts for the differences among human beings and things." And he ended by saying, "What is completely blocked cannot be penetrated, what is heavily blocked can be penetrated but doing so is difficult, and what is lightly blocked is easy to penetrate."[2]

Someone also asked: If a person routinely does what is not good and descends ever lower morally, in the end can he ever return to his original nature?

Zhu replied: When the tendency becomes extreme, he cannot return. But it will also depend on the depth of his knowledge and the abundance of his effort. (4.57)

2. Someone asked: The principle of heaven and earth endowed in each thing and person constitutes their natures; and the psychophysical stuff they all receive from heaven and earth constitutes their form. The differences in people's quality is owing to the differences in the clarity and abundance of their psychophysical stuff. As for things, I do not know whether their differences are because the principle they receive is not whole or because the turbidity of their psychophysical stuff obscures it.

Zhu replied: It's only because they receive a certain psychophysical stuff that they have a certain principle. Take dogs and horses: because their bodily psychophysical stuff is as it is, they are only capable of doing certain things.

There was a further question: Each and every thing contains the one supreme ultimate [*taiji* 太極],* so isn't it that their principle is always complete?

He replied: It's fine to say they are whole, and it's also fine to call them one-sided. If we speak in terms of principle, they are whole; if we speak in terms of psychophysical stuff, they are unavoidably one-sided. That is why Yushu [Lü Dalin]³ said that there are cases where the nature of a thing is close to the nature of a human being and cases where the nature of a human being is close to the nature of a thing. (4.57)

3. Someone asked: Aren't the differences in turbidity of the psychophysical material owing to the wholeness or one-sidedness of the nature decreed by heaven?

Zhu replied: It isn't that there is wholeness or one-sidedness. Let's say it is like the light of the sun or the moon: if you are on open ground, you will have a full view of it. If you are in a thatched room there will be places where the light is blocked, so you will view it only here and there. The turbidity is on account of the psychophysical stuff being turbid and so the nature is naturally blocked—it's like being in a thatched room. But, in people, what is blocked can be penetrated. As far as beasts go, they too have this nature, but it is constrained by their bodies. They are born with extreme blockage—there is no place where it can be penetrated. When it comes to the benevolence of tigers and wolves, the ceremoniousness of jackals and otters, and the righteousness of bees and ants, it is simply that there is a little penetration, like a crack of light. When it comes to monkeys, their appearance is

---

*The term "supreme ultimate" is found in a number of early classical texts. But Zhou Dunyi, in the early Song, would make it the basis of his philosophical system and describe it as the oneness before duality, from which yin and yang, the five phases, and the myriad things emerged. Zhu incorporates the supreme ultimate into his system and frequently identifies it with principle.

like humans' and so they are the most intelligent (*ling*) of all creatures—they just can't talk. When it comes to barbarians, they are somewhere between man and beasts and so in the end very difficult to reform. (4.58)

4.   Someone said: The nature of man and things is the same.

Zhu replied: The nature of man and things originally is the same, it's just that the endowment of the psychophysical stuff is different. It's like water, which is always clear. Pour it into a white bowl and it assumes that color, pour it into a black bowl and it assumes that color, pour it into a green bowl and it assumes that color. He added: Nature is most difficult to talk about. If you want to say it's the same, you can; if you want to say it's different, you can. It's like the sunlight shining through cracks: the cracks are naturally different sizes, but it's all still the same sunlight. (4.58)

5.   Between heaven and earth it is not only human beings who are most intelligent. Our mind-heart is the mind-heart of birds and beasts, grass and trees, but it is humans alone who are born perfectly balanced between heaven and earth. (4.59)

6.   Someone asked: People and things are different owing to the capacity of their psychophysical endowments. But how about grass and trees?

Zhu replied: The psychophysical stuff of grass and trees is also different: it has absolutely no faculty for knowing. (4.60)

7.   Grasses and trees all get yin psychophysical stuff; land animals and birds all get yang psychophysical stuff. Each of these can be further categorized. Grasses gets yin psychophysical stuff and trees get yang psychophysical stuff—and so grass is soft and trees are hard. Land animals get yin psychophysical stuff, and birds get yang psychophysical stuff. And so land animals lie in the grass and birds perch in the trees. But some land animals also get yang psychophysical stuff, like monkeys, and some birds get yin psychophysical stuff, like chickens and birds of prey. So, yes,

while grasses and trees all get yin psychophysical stuff, there are some where yang is within the yin and somewhere yin is within the yang. (4.62)

B. PRINCIPLE AND PSYCHOPHYSICAL STUFF IN HUMANS

8. A person is produced by nothing more than the convergence of principle and psychophysical stuff. Heavenly principle is incredibly vast and limitless, so if there weren't this psychophysical stuff, though this principle would exist, it would have nothing to which to attach itself. Thus, it is essential that the yin and yang psychophysical stuff interact and merge into one. Only then does principle have something to which to adhere. That human beings can talk and move, deliberate and act, is all a matter of psychophysical stuff; principle resides within it. Thus, when people manifest filiality, brotherliness, loyalty, trustworthiness, true goodness, righteousness, propriety, and wisdom—this is all a matter of principle. Because the yin and yang psychophysical stuff and the five elements interact in a myriad of variations, people and things are born with differences in degree of refinement. As for the primordial psychophysical stuff: all people and things receive this psychophysical stuff and are born; as for their degree of refinement, people receive psychophysical stuff that is upright and unobstructed, while things receive psychophysical stuff that is one-sided and blocked. Only people get the upright psychophysical stuff and, as a result, their principle is unobstructed—nowhere is it blocked. Things get one-sided psychophysical stuff and, as a result, their principle is blocked and they are insentient. Let's consider people: [As the *Huainanzi* explains], their heads are round in the image of heaven and their feet are square in the image of earth. They are balanced and proper. And because they receive the upright psychophysical stuff of heaven and earth, they know the principle of the Way and have

the capacity for understanding. Things receive one-sided psychophysical stuff from heaven and earth. And so beasts live in a horizontal position, vegetation lives with the head [the root] at the bottom and the limbs [the branches] turned upward. Some things have the capacity for understanding, but their understanding may operate in one area only: birds understand filial piety, otters understand reverence, dogs are capable only of protection, and oxen are capable only of plowing and nothing else. In the case of people, there's nothing they don't understand, nothing they're incapable of. The reason for the difference between people and things is simply this discrepancy [that is, in the different allotments of psychophysical stuff]. Still, speaking of people's allotment: there are also differences of dark and bright, clear and turbid. The psychophysical endowment of the "most wise,"[4] and of "those born knowing it,"[5] is clear, bright, and pure, without the slightest turbidity; that is why they are capable of knowing it at birth and practicing it effortlessly, without having to learn, as in the case of Yao and Shun. Next, and inferior to "born knowing it," are those who have to learn it to know it[6] and attain to it with effort. Still next are those whose allotment is one-sided and concealing, and where arduous effort is required. "What a person can do in one try, he will dedicate one hundred tries to; what a person can do in ten tries, he will dedicate a thousand tries to."[7] Only then is he able to catch up to those who come right after those born knowing it. If he advances without stop, his results will be the same as theirs. The *Mencius* says, "Slight is the difference between humans and beast."[8] The reason for the difference between humans and things is this little discrepancy [i.e., in allotments of psychophysical stuff]. If we do not hold on to it there is no difference between us and beasts. When I was fifteen or sixteen I read the paragraph in the *Mean*, "What a person can do in one try, he will dedicate one hundred tries to; what a person can do in ten tries, he will dedicate a thousand tries to"[9] and then came across Lü Yushu [Lü Dalin]'s splendid explanation of the section.[10] Whenever I read the passage from the *Mean*, I shudder and feel ever more vigilant and inspired. If a person has the determination to learn, it is essential that he make this sort of effort if he is to be successful. (4.65)

9. Nature is just principle. Without heaven's psychophysical stuff and earth's materiality (*zhi*), this principle has no place to settle. If the psychophysical stuff is clear and bright then there will be no obstruction and principle will issue forth smoothly. If there is little obstruction, it will issue forth, and heavenly principle will triumph. If the obstruction is great, then selfish desires will triumph. From this it is evident that the original nature has nothing that is not good. This is what Mencius meant by "the nature being good," what Zhou [Dunyi] meant by "unadulterated good," and what Master Cheng meant by "original nature" and the nature implied in his phrases "returning to the origin" and "tracing to the source." (4.66)

10. When we speak of the nature of heaven and earth [*tiandi zhi xing* 天地之性] this refers solely to principle. When we speak of the psychophysical nature [*qizhi zhi xing* 氣質之性] this refers to the combination of principle and psychophysical stuff. Before this psychophysical stuff exists, this nature already exists. And while psychophysical stuff may not be preserved, the nature, by contrast, always exists. Even though it lies squarely within the psychophysical stuff, the psychophysical stuff is nonetheless psychophysical stuff and the nature is the nature, and they do not mix. If we talk about its being embodied in things, nature exists everywhere: and no matter how coarse the psychophysical stuff, principle is sure to exist. (4.67)

11. Human nature is principle. And principle as it ought to be is wholly good. Therefore, when Mencius spoke of human

nature he spoke of original nature. But to establish itself it has to cleave to something and hence the psychophysical endowment, which cannot but have differences in quality and quantity. (4.67)

12. In the universe, there is just the one principle of the Way. Human nature is principle. That some people are good and some are bad is owing simply to the difference in clarity of their psychophysical endowments. (4.68)

13. Every person's nature is good. But that some people at birth are good and some people at birth are evil is because their psychophysical endowments are different. Consider that heaven and earth revolve without beginning or end. And what is clear, without question, is that when people are born during times when the sun and moon are clear and bright and the weather is pleasant, they are endowed with the psychophysical stuff of the times, psychophysical stuff that is clean and bright and just, and this necessarily makes for a good person; but if the sun and moon are dim and dark and the weather abnormal, this is the perverse psychophysical stuff of heaven and earth—and when people are endowed with it, it makes for an evil person. People engage in learning because they want to transform the psychophysical stuff, but it is extremely hard to transform it. Mencius, for instance, spoke of the nature being good but said nothing of the psychophysical endowment; he said only that "all men could become a Yao or Shun." For him, if a person advances boldly, the one-sidedness of his psychophysical endowment will naturally dissipate and his efforts will naturally pay off. Thus, he did not speak about the psychophysical endowment. If we look into why we are unable to become sages and worthies given that our nature is already good, it's that we are impaired by the psychophysical endowment. If, for instance, the psychophysical endowment is one-sidedly unyielding, we will be the type inclined toward violence; but if it is one-sidedly pliant, we'll be the type inclined toward weakness. A person who offers the excuse that

his psychophysical endowment is bad and does nothing about it, will benefit not at all; and one who leaves unexamined the harm caused by the psychophysical endowment and wanders about in a muddle, likewise, will not benefit at all. Having acknowledged the harm caused by the psychophysical endowment, we need to work hard to bring it under control, master it, and return it to a balanced state—then we'll be fine. (4.69)

14. Daofu asked: With whom did talk of the psychophysical material begin?

Zhu replied: It started with Zhang [Zai] and the Cheng [brothers]. I believe that utmost effort should be devoted to the teachings of the disciples of Confucius, supplemented by the teachings of later followers in the school. In reading, let people be especially inspired by Zhang and the Cheng brothers as no one before them spoke of the psychophysical material. In his essay "An Inquiry on Human Nature," Han Tuizhi [Han Yu] spoke of the three grades. What he said was correct, but he never spoke clearly about the psychophysical nature—only that human nature had three grades. Mencius said that human nature is good, but he was speaking of its original aspect. Never did he speak of the psychophysical nature that follows, leaving it unexplained. The various schools of thought said that human nature is bad or a mix of good and bad; if the explanations of Zhang and the Cheng brothers had appeared earlier, these various explanations would not have been so confused. And so when the explanations of Zhang and the Chengs became established, the explanations by the various philosophers fell into neglect. (4.70)

15. The nature is like water: if it flows through a clear channel, it is clear; if it flows through a dirty channel, it is turbid. When clear or upright psychophysical stuff receives it, it is whole; such is the case with human beings. When turbid or one-sided psychophysical stuff gets it, it is obscured; such is the case with beasts. Psychophysical stuff is clear or turbid: human beings

receive clear stuff, and beasts receive turbid stuff. And because human beings, in general, are basically clear, they differ from beasts. At the same time, there are those with turbid stuff and so they are not very different from beasts. (4.73)

16. There exists this principle and then there exists this psychophysical stuff; and once this psychophysical stuff exists, this principle necessarily exists. Those endowed with clear psychophysical stuff are sages and worthies, whose principle is like a precious pearl lying in crystal-clear water; and those endowed with turbid psychophysical stuff are idiots and degenerates whose principle is like a pearl lying in turbid water. What we call "keeping the inborn luminous virtue unobscured"[11] is to reach into the turbid water and wipe clean this pearl. (4.73)

17. Principle rests in psychophysical stuff just as a pearl rests in water. Principle resting in clear psychophysical stuff will, like a pearl resting in clean water, be thoroughly bright; principle resting in turbid psychophysical stuff will, like a pearl resting in turbid water, not shine bright.

Someone asked: If there is something profoundly obstructing it, while there may be a pearl there, it's as if it's deep in mud and can't be grasped.

Zhu replied: The same is true of principle. (4.73).

18. Someone asked about psychophysical endowments having different degrees of clarity and turbidity.

Zhu replied: There is more than this one kind of difference in the psychophysical endowment: it is not just a matter of the two words "clarity" and "turbidity." Some people today have a quick intelligence and understand everything—their psychophysical stuff is clear. But they do not necessarily always accord with principle because their psychophysical stuff is not "pure." There are those who are respectful, generous, devoted, and trustworthy—their psychophysical stuff is pure. But they do not necessarily always succeed in aligning with principle because their psychophysical stuff is not clear. Ponder this while pursing the matter, and it will be obvious. (4.74)

19. Even though human nature is the same, the psychophysical stuff we are endowed with can't but have imbalances. There are those who receive a heavy load of "wood" psychophysical stuff [with "wood" referring to one of five phases in which psychophysical stuff manifests] and whose mind-heart of compassion is constantly great, but whose mind-hearts of shame, courtesy and modesty, and right and wrong[12] are obstructed by the wood psychophysical stuff and do not become manifest. There are those who receive a heavy load of "metal" psychophysical stuff and whose mind-heart of shame is constantly great but whose mind-hearts of compassion, courtesy and modesty, and right and wrong are obstructed by the metal psychophysical stuff and do not become manifest. It's the same with water and fire. Only when yin and yang unite in virtue and the five natures are perfectly complete will there be true balance and a person become a sage. (4.74)

20. "The Master said, 'By nature near together, in practice far apart.'"[13] What is called nature here is spoken of in combination with psychophysical stuff. In the psychophysical nature, there are indeed differences of good and bad. And yet if we speak of the very beginning, people's psychophysical natures are not far apart at all. It is simply that people practice good and so become good, or practice bad and so become bad. Only thus do they grow apart.[14]

21. Yafu said: Nature is like the sun and the moon; the turbidity of the psychophysical stuff is like clouds and fog. The Master thought this to be the case. (4.76)

22. There was a question: What is the difference between nature [*xing*] and decree [*ming* 命]?

Zhu replied: Nature speaks of principle; decree speaks of principle combined with psychophysical stuff. Decree has differences in amount and weight, while nature is the same in all. And this principle, in a sage, a dullard, a worthy, or a miscreant, is all the same. (4.77)

23. There was a question: The Master rarely spoke of decree [*ming*].[15] As for true goodness, righteousness, propriety, and wisdom and the five constant virtues, they are all decreed by heaven. Why is it that what is decreed for social position, wealth, living and dying, and life span are different?

Zhu replied: All of these are what heaven decrees. To receive refined and vigorous psychophysical stuff is to become a sage or worthy—it is to get principle whole and upright. Those who receive clear and bright stuff are vigorous and quick. Those who receive sincere stuff are temperate. Those who receive clear and exalted stuff are noble. Those who receive abundant stuff are wealthy. Those who receive extended stuff live a long life. Those who receive decaying and ailing stuff become stupid, worthless, impoverished, humble, and die young. Heaven gives birth to people with certain psychophysical stuff and a great many things follow from it. He added: What heaven decrees is indeed equal. But when it comes to the psychophysical endowments, they are not the same. Let's consider how the endowments work. When the endowment is generous, the principle of the Way is complete. I have talked about the decree before. It is like an imperial order from the court. The mind-heart is like an official, appointed by the court to serve as an official. Human nature is like the duties of the official: a prefect has the duties of a prefect and the district magistrate has the duties of a district magistrate, but their official duties are of the same kind—to instruct the people born of heaven in the multitudinous manifestations of the principle of the Way and to delegate to them their various duties. The psychophysical endowment is like the official emolument. The noble stuff is like that for a high-ranking official and the base stuff is like that for a low-ranking official; the abundant stuff is like a generous emolument and the impoverished stuff is like a slight emolument; the stuff for long life is like a two-to three-year official appointment that comes to an and is then renewed, and the stuff for a short life is like an appointment that isn't served out to the end. The court appoints a person to serve as an official and many things all at once follow from it. Hengqu [Zhang Zai] said, "After something forms it has its psychophysical nature. If the good overcomes it, the nature of heaven and earth will be preserved. Thus, the superior person does not take the psychophysical nature to be his nature."[16] A psychophysical endowment that is clear and bright will have this principle of the Way within it. One that is dark and turbid will as well; the principle of the Way will simply be within it, just blocked by the dark and turbid stuff. It's like water: when it is clear, even the tiniest thing in it is visible, but when it is murky it isn't. When Mencius said that human nature is good, he was looking at what is most essential and was not speaking of the psychophysical nature in all of its particulars. Master Cheng said, "To discuss nature without discussing psychophysical stuff is incomplete. To discuss psychophysical stuff without discussing nature is unclear. To treat them as two separate things is incorrect."[17] Mencius only discussed nature without discussing psychophysical stuff, so his discussion was not entirely complete. And if we discuss nature without discussing psychophysical stuff, we are not treating the original character of nature thoroughly. Xun[zi], Yang [Xiong, 53 BCE–18 CE], Han [Yu], and others, though they discussed human nature, in fact were only speaking of psychophysical stuff. Xunzi merely looked at the nature of bad people and thus said it was bad; Master Yang looked at people where it was half good and half bad and so said it was a mix of good and bad; Master Han looked at the many kinds of people in the world and therefore established his theory of the three grades. Of these three philosophers, Master Han's theory came closest. He regarded true goodness, righteous, propriety, and wisdom as the nature, and pleasure, anger, sorrow, and joy as the emotions. The weakness in it, though, is the rare use of the word "psychophysical stuff." (4.77)

24. Lüzhi said, "The Master is cordial yet stern, awe-inspiring yet not fierce, respectful yet at ease,"[18] and then he asked: Those who receive clear, bright psychophysical stuff become sages or worthies, those who receive dark, turbid psychophysical stuff become stupid and worthless. Those with abundant psychophysical stuff become wealthy and noble and those with slight psychophysical stuff become impoverished and humble. This, to be sure, is the case. But the Sage [i.e., Confucius] received heaven and earth's clear, bright, and harmonious psychophysical stuff, and presumably had no deficiency, yet contrarily the Master was poor and lowly. Why was that? Was it luck that made this so or was it that his endowment was, in fact, lacking?

Zhu replied: What he was endowed with was lacking. That clarity and brightness of his psychophysical stuff simply determined that he become a sage or worthy but did not determine wealth or status. Those who receive exalted stuff will be noble, those who receive abundant stuff will be wealthy, those who receive extended stuff will live a long life. For the poor, lowly, and short-lived the converse is the case. While the Master got the clear and bright stuff and thus became a sage, he was nonetheless endowed with the lowly and slight stuff and so became poor and humble. Yanzi [Yan Hui 顏回]† was different from Confucius. He was endowed with shortened stuff and so died young.

Someone also asked: [In the phrase] "one yin, one yang, alternating,"[19] there appears to be an even mix. So worthy and unworthy people ought to be balanced in number. Why is it then that morally superior people (*junzi* 君子) are always few and "small men" always numerous?

---

†Yan Hui was Confucius's most gifted disciple.

Zhu replied: It's natural that people's stuff is mixed. How are they to achieve the right balance? Let's compare it to forging metal coins. Unalloyed ones are always rare and alloyed ones are always numerous. It's natural that their psychophysical stuff is mixed. But [when coins are forged] some psychophysical stuff comes to the fore, and some falls to the back, so getting just the right mix is impossible. How can just the right composition be achieved? Or let's compare it to days: some are yin, some are yang, some are windy, some are rainy; some are cold, some are hot; some are clear and comfortable, some are oppressive. And on any given day there can be many changes. From this we can understand.

Someone further asked: But while it's a mix, in the end it's nothing but yin and yang psychophysical stuff, so where does the inequality come in?

Zhu replied: It isn't like this. If it were just a matter of two individuated entities, yin and yang, then there would be no inequality. But because stuff mixes together in a myriad variety, achieving just the right balance between the two is not possible.

There was another question: If this is the case, isn't it that heaven and earth produce sages and worthies by chance and without intentionality?

Zhu replied: Where did heaven and earth ever say, "we particularly want to produce a sage or worthy?" It's simply that the psychophysical stuff in that spot comes together in just the right way and thereby produces a sage or worthy. And when he is born it just seems as if it was heaven's intention.

There was still another question: Kangjie [Shao Yong] said, "One yang to two yins—this is why superior persons are few and 'small men' many." Is this right?

Zhu replied: You can say that. It's natural that there is little good stuff and an abundance of bad stuff. It's like the previous matters, where similarly the good were few and the bad abundant. The principle is the same. (4.79)

25. Human nature is principle. In the mind-heart it is called human nature; in things it is called principle. (5.82)

26. Human nature is how we should be. (5.83)

27. Human nature is purely the good. (5.83)

28. Human nature is principle. True goodness, righteousness, propriety, and wisdom are all contained therein. (5.83)

29. Human nature is not some distinct thing that appears before us. Just probe principle [*giong li* 窮理] and investigate things [*gewu*][20] and human nature will be found therein—no need to seek after it. For this reason, the sages rarely spoke of human nature. (5.83)

C. The Mind-Heart: Where Human Nature and Emotions Meet

30. Someone asked: Is the seat of spiritual efficacy [*ling*] the mind-heart or human nature?

Zhu replied: The seat of spiritual efficacy is just the mind-heart, not human nature. Human nature is just principle. (5.85)

31. Someone asked: Is consciousness the spiritual efficacy [*ling*] of the mind-heart being what it is? Or is it the activity of the psychophysical stuff?

Zhu replied: It's not solely the psychophysical stuff, for first there must be the principle of consciousness. Principle is not consciousness. Psychophysical stuff gathers and takes shape, principle and psychophysical stuff unite, and then consciousness is possible. It can be likened to a candle flame: it's owing to the candle fat that this flame exists.

Another question: The locus of the mind-heart's activity is the psychophysical stuff, right?

Zhu said: Yes, it's simply consciousness. (5.85)

32. The object of consciousness is principle. Principle is not separate from consciousness and consciousness is not separate from principle. (5.85)

33. Someone asked: The mind-heart is consciousness and the nature is principle. How do they interpenetrate and become one?

Zhu replied: No need for them to make any effort to interpenetrate, for they interpenetrate from the very beginning.

How is it that they interpenetrate at the beginning?

Zhu said: If principle has no mind-heart, it has nothing to adhere to. (5.85)

34. The object of our consciousness is the principle in our mind-heart. What allows for consciousness is the spiritual efficacy of the psychophysical stuff. (5.85)

35. The mind-heart is the refined and agile psychophysical stuff. (5.85)

36. Someone asked: All principles are complete in the entity of the mind-heart. The good that issues forth indeed arises from the mind-heart. As for the bad that issues forth, isn't this the selfishness of creaturely desires of the psychophysical endowment, which likewise arises from the mind?

Zhu replied: It isn't the original substance of the mind-heart, but it does arise from the mind-heart.

Someone further asked: This is the so-called mind-heart of man?

Yes.

Zisheng thereupon asked: Does the mind-heart of man also mix good and evil?

Zhu replied: Yes, you can say they're mixed. (5.86)

37. Someone asked: Does the mind-heart have good and evil?

Zhu replied: The mind-heart is an active entity and naturally has good and evil. For instance, compassion is good; but when a person sees a child fall into a well and is devoid of a mind-heart of compassion, this is evil.[21] Departing from goodness is evil. And so while the original substance of the mind-heart is always good, you can't say that evil has nothing at all to do with the mind-heart. For if it isn't the mind-heart, what is it that departs from goodness? The learning of the ancients asks us to probe

principle and extend knowledge, and forthwith make the effort
to reduce evil so that goodness gradually returns on its own. To
take hold and preserve [the mind-heart] is something that happens later, not at a time when there are both good and evil. (5.86)

38. Someone asked: Is the movement of the body related to
the mind-heart?

Zhu replied: How could they be unrelated! It's the mind-heart
that naturally orders it to move. (5.86)

39. Human nature is like the supreme ultimate [*taiji*] and the
mind-heart is like yin and yang. The supreme ultimate is simply
within the yin and yang and incapable of separating from yin and
yang. Still, to talk about the supreme ultimate is to talk about
the supreme ultimate itself and to talk about yin and yang is to
talk about yin/yang itself. This is also the case with human nature
and the mind-heart. This is the so-called one and yet two, two
and yet one. Master Han [Yu] used true goodness, righteousness,
propriety, wisdom, and trustworthiness to speak of human nature
and pleasure, anger, sorrow, and joy to speak of emotions. He
went further than others in speaking of human nature, and yet
in analyzing the "three grades" he was still talking only of psychophysical stuff, not of human nature. (5.87)

40. Human nature is the principle contained in the mind-
heart; the mind-heart is the place where principle gathers. (5.88)

41. Although the mind-heart is a distinct thing, it is empty
and so is able to embody the multitudinous manifestations of
principle. (5.88)

42. Human nature is principle. The mind-heart is what
embraces and sustains it, issuing it forth into operation. (5.88)

43. The mind-heart has good and evil. The nature is entirely
good. If we talk about the psychophysical nature, it indeed has
that which isn't good. (5.89)

44. By explaining and by naming we can understand clearly.
Take mind-heart and nature, both difficult to explain. I've said:

The nature is the principle in the mind-heart. The emotions are the movement of the human nature. And the mind-heart is the master of the nature and the emotions. (5.89)

45. We have this nature, and it issues forth these emotions. If you trace these emotions back, you will discover this nature; and if you trace your emotions today, you will discover that you had this nature originally. (5.89)

46. We can't describe human nature itself. When we describe the nature as good it's simply because we see the goodness in our commiseration and complaisance and the other four germs[†] and from *this* can know the goodness of human nature. It's like when we see clear flowing water; we know that its source must be clear. The four germs are the emotions, and nature is principle. What issues forth are the emotions; their source is human nature. It's like when we see a shadow; we have a good idea of the form itself. (5.89)

47. Someone asked about mind-heart, emotions, and human nature.

Zhu replied: The section in the *Mencius* where he said, "The mind-heart of compassion is the germ of true goodness" is extremely clear. Compassion, shame, right and wrong, and humility and deference are the emotions that issue forth; goodness, righteousness, propriety, and wisdom are the substance of human nature. There simply exist within human nature true goodness, righteousness, propriety, and wisdom; issuing forth they constitute compassion, humility and deference, right and wrong—the emotions of human nature. People today speak of human nature often saying, as the Buddhists and Daoists do, that separately there exists this thing somewhere, mysterious and wonderful,

---

[†]According to *Mencius* 2A.6, every human being is born with the germs of true goodness, righteousness, propriety, and wisdom, which constitute our good human nature.

and having spoken raptly of it then enter into the realm of emptiness and extinction. We Confucians do not go on about human
nature this way. Master Cheng said, "Human nature is principle."
These words are absolutely perfect. In the phrase "Mencius says
that human nature is good,"[22] the good is the human nature that
corresponds to the principle of the Way. This being the case, we
must we carefully come to understand the goodness for ourselves
and not simply accept the word of others. If we are vigilant in our
efforts and vigilant in our investigation, we will naturally understand. People today have no understanding at all—as soon as they
hear some ordinary fellow's wild ideas, they just go along. (5.92)

48. Someone asked about human nature, emotions, mind-
heart, and true goodness.

Zhu replied: Hengqu [Zhang Zai] explained it best, saying,
"the mind-heart governs the nature and the emotions." Mencius
said that the mind-heart of compassion is the germ of true goodness and the mind-heart that is ashamed of evil in oneself and
hates it in others is the germ of righteousness. This explains
human nature, emotions, and mind-heart better than anything.
Human nature is entirely good, but what issues forth from the
mind-heart are emotions, which sometimes are not good. To say
that such lack of goodness is not a matter of the mind-heart would
be wrong. For although the basic substance of the mind-heart is
originally perfectly good, when the mind-heart encounters what
is not good the emotions are misled by things. Human nature is
a general term for principle; and true goodness, righteousness,
propriety, and wisdom are all terms for the one principle within
human nature. Compassion, shame, right and wrong, and humility are terms for what issues forth from the emotions, and these
emotions, which arise from human nature, are good. What these
germs issue forth is extremely subtle and all arise from this mind-
heart. And thus it is said, "The mind-heart governs the human
nature and the emotions." Human nature is not a separate entity

in the mind-heart, for the mind-heart contains this human nature and the emotions. If the mind-heart loses its master there are times when it will not be good. Consider: "If I desire true goodness, true goodness would be right at hand."[23] If I desire not to be truly good, I will lose this true goodness. Or "Hui! For three months, he did not depart from true goodness."[24] To say that he did not depart from goodness for three months means that the mind-heart sometimes *does* depart from true goodness. Or, "It comes and goes at no appointed times and no one knows where it will settle."[25] Preserve it, concentrating on but one thing at a time so that you do not lose it—and it will be good. The essence of this is found in the "extension of knowledge," and the extension of knowledge rests in probing principle.[26] When principle is probed, knowledge naturally reaches its highest point. Best to examine the effort you put into learning and consider whether your knowledge has reached its highest point or not. It isn't that you need know everything and then some. With each affair, scrupulously investigate principle and after a while it will naturally appear bright to you. As with a mirror, if today you polish it a bit and then tomorrow you polish it a bit, it will grow brighter naturally without your noticing it. If it does grow brighter but your effort then ceases, it will become the dusty mirror it was before— the places where it had grown brighter will darken and the places where it had yet to brighten will not recover their [original] brightness. (5.92)

49. As for human nature, emotions, and the mind-heart, only Mencius and Hengqu [Zhang Zai] alone explained them well. True goodness is human nature; compassion is an emotion, which necessarily issues from the mind-heart. "The mind-and-heart governs the nature and the emotions." Human nature is merged with emotions in this way. It is simply principle and not some separate entity. If it were something with its own existence, it would necessarily possess evil in addition to goodness. But it isn't

such a thing. It is because it is principle alone that it is entirely good. (5. 93)

50. The two lines, Cheng Yichuan's [Cheng Yi's] "nature is principle" and Zhang Hengqu's [Zhang Zai's] "the mind-heart governs the nature and the emotions" are eternal! (5.93)

51. Human nature is an inactive state; the emotions are an active state. The mind-heart embodies both the inactive and active states. It would seem that the inactive state of the mind-heart constitutes human nature and the active state constitutes the emotions, which is what is meant by "the mind-heart governs the nature and the emotions." Desire issues forth from emotions. The mind-heart is like water, human nature is like the tranquility of water, emotions are like the flow of the water, and desires are like the waters' waves. Some waves are good and some are bad. Good desires are of the "I desire true goodness" sort. Bad ones are those that rush ahead forcefully, like great, crashing waves. For the most part, the bad ones overwhelm heavenly principle. It's like when water swells up—no place avoids damage. Mencius said that emotions can be good, which is to speak of those proper emotions that flow out from human nature. Originally, they're all good. (5.93)

52. The mind-heart refers to the master. In both movement and stillness it is the master. It isn't that in stillness it does not operate, and only with movement becomes the master. If we speak of the master, it is an integrated hub that naturally resides within us. The mind-heart governs the nature and the emotions. It is not some incomplete thing that becomes one with the nature and the emotions and is indistinguishable from them. (5.94)

53. The mind-heart is master of the nature and operates through the emotions. Therefore [as the *Mean* says], "Before pleasure, anger, sorrow, and joy have arisen—this we call perfect balance. After they have arisen and attained due proportion— this we call harmony."[27] The mind-heart is the seat of the effort here. (5.94)

54. The whole substance of the mind-heart is calm, unprejudiced, and bright. The myriad manifestations of principle are complete therein. It is without the slightest selfish desire. It flows everywhere, pervading movement and stillness. There is no place where its wondrous operations are not found. Thus, when it is not yet active and is whole in substance, we speak of it as human nature; when it has become active and wondrous in its operations, we speak of it as emotions. And so "the mind-heart governs the nature and the emotions." Only from the perspective of the integrated whole do we speak of the still "inactive" and the already "active." It isn't that human nature is one particular locale, the mind-heart another, and emotions still another, with distance separating one from the other. (5.94)

55. Someone asked about the distinctions between the mind-heart, the nature, and the emotions.

Zhu replied: Master Cheng said, "The mind-heart can be compared to a grain seed: the principle for production within it is its nature and when its yang psychophysical stuff sends forth shoots that's its emotion. This, by extension, is the case with all things."²⁸ (5.95)

56. Someone asked: Aren't the intentions (*yi* 意) the operations of the mind-heart—that is, what issues forth from it?

Zhu replied: When it operates, they issue forth.

A further question: Don't the emotions (*qing*) issue forth as well? If so, how do they differ?

Zhu said: Emotions are activated by human nature (*xing*). Emotions issue forth from it. Intentions express what it is that one desires. For instance, the love of a particular thing is an emotion; choosing to love a particular thing is an intention. Emotions are like a boat or cart. Intentions are like a person wanting to make use of the boat or cart. (5.95)

57. To be inactive but capable of activity is principle. To be inactive but desiring to be active is intention (*yi*). (5.96)

58. Where the mind-heart is headed is called the will.²⁹ (5.96)

59. Someone asked about "intention" and "ambition."

Zhu replied: Hengqu [Zhang Zai] said, "When we speak of these two words, 'intention' and 'ambition,' ambition is public and intention is private, ambition is hard and intention is soft, ambition is yang and intention is yin." (5.96).

60. "Ambition" is to express publicly what one wants to do; "intention" is manifest privately and in secret. Ambition is like an open attack; intention is like a raid. (5.96)

61. Substance (*ti* 體) is this principle; function (*yong* 用) is the operation. For example, that the ear hears and the eyes see is naturally the case—this is principle. Opening the eyes to see things and pricking the ears to hear sounds—this is function. (6.101)

62. What people simply ought to do is substance. The aspect of doing is function. It can be compared to a fan. It has a monture and a handle, and it is made of paper and paste—this is its substance. People wave it—this is its function. (6.102)

63. Someone asked: Last year I heard the Master say, "There is but one principle of the Way; its manifestations are different." Isn't what you mean by "different" that principle is one but its functions are different—as in the goodness of a lord, the reverence of a minister, the filiality of a child, the affection of a father, and the trustworthiness in relations with countrymen?

Zhu replied: The substances (*ti*) themselves are already somewhat different. The relationships between ruler and minister, father and son, and countrymen are the substance. True goodness, reverence, affection, filiality, and trustworthiness are the functions.

Someone asked: Substances and functions are all different?

Zhu replied: Take this board: there's just one principle of the Way, but this grain goes this way and that grain goes that way. Or take this house: there's just one principle of the Way, but there are different rooms. Or take the trees: there's just one principle of the Way, but there's the peach tree and there's the plum tree.

Or take humankind: there's just one principle of the Way, but there is the third son of Zhang and the fourth son of Li. The fourth son of Li can't become the third son of Zhang and the third son of Zhang can't become the fourth son of Li. Or take yin and yang: the *Western Inscription* [by Zhang Zai] explains that their "principle is one but their manifestations are many." (6.102)

64. Authenticity (*cheng*) is truly to possess this principle. (6.102)

65. Authenticity is simply to be true [to principle]. He added: authenticity is principle. (6.102)

66. *Cheng* ("authenticity") is "to be true to principle;" it's also "to be sincere." Ever since the Han dynasty, *cheng* has been explained exclusively as "sincere." With Master Cheng, for the first time, it was explained as "being true to principle." Later scholars have abandoned the explanation of "sincere," paying no heed to the fact that *The Mean* sometimes explains *cheng* as "being true to principle" and sometimes as "being sincere." We must not simply regard "being true" as *cheng* and "being sincere" as not *cheng*. (6.102)

67. The Master asked the gathering, "What is the difference between reverential attentiveness and authenticity?"

Everyone responded by citing the words of Master Cheng. The Master said, "Reverential attentiveness means do not be undisciplined and authenticity means do not be deceptive." (6.103)

68. To be false and deceptive is to be inauthentic (*bucheng* 不誠). To be lazy and undisciplined is to be inattentive (*bujing* 不敬). This is the difference between authenticity and reverential attentiveness. (6.103)

69. The word "caution" (*jin* 謹) does not compare to "reverential attentiveness," and "reverential attentiveness" does not compare to "authenticity." Master Cheng said, "To concentrate on one thing is what is meant by reverential attentiveness. And oneness is what is meant by authenticity."[30] In being reverentially attentive we still need to exert ourselves. (6.103)

70. Someone asked, True goodness is what we receive first. I gather we can say that true goodness is possessed of righteousness, propriety, and wisdom?

Zhu replied: First there is this principle of life [i.e., true goodness]; the other three emanate from it. (6.107)

71. Students must seek true goodness. To seek true goodness means not to lose this mind-heart of ours.[31] The Sage too simply taught people to seek true goodness. As for true goodness, righteousness, propriety, and wisdom—the four virtues—it seems that true goodness sufficiently embodies them all. If you're able to hold on to true goodness, you will naturally do things in an orderly manner without any contriving. Thus, it is said, "'If you set your mind-heart on true goodness,'[32] there will be no evil." As you read the *Greater Learning* you need to recognize this idea in the passage: "[Tang's] attention was constantly on his heaven-given luminous Virtue."[33] [As Mencius said], "There's nothing else but to seek for the lost mind-heart.[34] (6.113)

72. Someone asked: Is to preserve this mind-heart to be truly good?

Zhu replied: You need to preserve this mind-heart and not allow it to be overcome by selfish desires. In everything, remain mentally alert and in control—do not simply go along with things. You must hold on to it tightly. If you preserve this mind-heart at all times, no matter the situation or thing you encounter, though you may not get it exactly right you will not be far off. If your thoughts are confused you will be incapable of preserving this mind-heart, and if the mind isn't preserved, you will not know to look where you ought to look and you won't know to listen when you ought to listen. (6.114)

73. Clear out all selfish desires and heavenly principle will flow forth. This is to be truly good. (6.117)

74. Yu Zhengshu[35] said: To be free of selfish desires is to be truly good. Zhu replied: It's okay to say that after we become free

of selfish desires, we become truly good; it's not okay to say that to be free of selfish desires is to be truly good. It seems that only when we become free of selfish desires does true goodness *start* to appear. It's like only when there's no blockage does water begin to flow.

Fangshu (Zhengshu's brother) said: To be of one body with heaven, earth, and the myriad things is to be truly good.

Zhu replied: "To be free of selfish desire" precedes true goodness and "to be of one with heaven, earth, and the myriad things" follows upon being truly good. Only when we are free of selfish desire do we become truly good and only when we are truly good do we become one with heaven, earth, and the myriad things. It is critical that given these two propositions we ultimately recognize what "true goodness" really exemplifies. If we are to be clear about the meaning of the term *ren*, "true goodness," we need to consider the three words, "righteousness," "propriety," and "wisdom." And if we really want to understand what true goodness exemplifies, we must try to "subdue the self and return to ritual."[36] People these days talk about true goodness the way they talk about candy: everyone says its sweet, but those who have never eaten it don't even know what sweetness tastes like. Sages never divulge too much—it's up to students to experience it for themselves. (6.117)

Human beings thus find themselves in a moral predicament. They live with the capability of being fully moral, yet mostly find themselves falling short of moral perfection. According to Zhu, every human being has the same innate moral potential but this potential has to be consciously and actively realized. For him, it is by refining and clarifying their psychophysical endowment that people enable the principle that is their originally good nature to shine forth. This is the purpose of learning and explains why it is at the heart of Zhu Xi's philosophical agenda.

Zhu is dismayed by what he sees as the learning typical of the day. The way of learning he advocates is intended to be a corrective. Inspired by a remark Confucius made in the *Analects* (14.24), he distinguishes between two antithetical kinds of learning: "learning for the sake of others" (為人之學) and "learning for the sake of oneself (為己之學). His contemporaries, he believes, are given to learning for the sake of others, by which he means learning intended primarily to impress others and win worldly recognition and wealth. Included here is learning done principally to achieve success in the civil service examinations and win official position and to garner literary and intellectual renown. The learning he proposes, by contrast, is "true learning"—learning that seeks moral improvement and self-transformation without calculation of worldly gain. This is learning for one's own sake, the learning done by the great sages and worthies of the past and transmitted to later generations in their writings.

Effective learning, Zhu Xi believed, should be sequential, in a program of graded learning, as it had been in antiquity. This explains, in part, why the Way had flourished in antiquity. At age eight, boys would enter the school of "lesser learning," where they received instruction in what Zhu referred to as "affairs." "Affairs" included activities intended to socialize a child, like cleaning and sweeping, polite conversation, and ritual; skills especially prized by the tradition, such as music, archery, charioteering, calligraphy, and mathematics; and the performance of classical virtues— filiality, fraternal respect, loyalty, and trustworthiness.

Then, sometime at age sixteen or so, boys would enter the school of "greater learning," which focused on "the principle behind these affairs" (7.125). There, according to Zhu's "Preface to the *Greater Learning in Chapters and Verses*," they were taught "the Way of probing principle, setting the mind in the right, cultivating oneself, and governing others."[1] Learning, he cautions, must not be allowed to become "unsystematic" or "piecemeal" (8.142). He remarks, "If we liken it to climbing a mountain, people mostly want to get to the highest point, not realizing that unless they're familiar with the lower points there will be no getting to the higher ones!" (8.142) This is the mistake Buddhists make, he claims, for they "speak only of penetration on the higher level and give little attention to learning on the lower level." (44.1140)

Zhu holds out hope that students who engage attentively in the right sort of learning might themselves become sages or worthies. It is possible, he declares, to be "an ordinary villager yesterday and today become a sage." (8.135) From beginning to end learning is to take understanding of principle as its aim. It is the way to access principle and realize the originally good nature: "In learning you want only to understand this one moral principle. Once this is understood completely, heavenly principle and human desire, righteousness and profit, and impartiality and selfishness will all be understood." (8.131)

Essential to proper learning is the proper effort. Students must have the "determination," the "will," and the "zeal" to learn. Then, they must ready their mind so that it might apprehend the principle in things clearly and objectively. It needs to be *xu* 虛, "open" or "unprejudiced," he says, by which he means freed of "preconceived ideas" and without external distractions. The refrain to "open the mind" and to "keep the mind open" that runs throughout his conversations with students indicates how crucial this step is for Zhu in preparing students to advance along the Way.

For all the emphasis that he places on learning, Zhu warns against it becoming an end in itself. Knowledge not coupled with action is "superficial," he insists, and suggests that sage learning that does not take as its aim sage behavior is not true learning: "The difference between the ordinary sort of learning and that of the sages and worthies is not hard to see. Sages and worthies are truly intent on action. When they talk about 'setting the mind in the right,' they truly want to set the mind in the right. . . . When students today talk about setting the mind in the right, they're but briefly mouthing the words 'setting the mind in the right.'" (8.133)

A. Lesser Learning and Greater Learning

1.   In instructing others, Confucius begins with what is central and has them practice it with purpose. After a while they are able on their own to appreciate the higher principle of the Way. This is what is meant by, "My studies lie low, my penetration rises high." (19.429)

2.   At an early age the ancients would enter the school for lesser learning where their instruction was limited to affairs [*shi* 事] such as ritual, music, archery, charioteering, calligraphy, and mathematics, as well as the affairs of filiality, fraternal respect, loyalty, and trustworthiness. At the age of sixteen or seventeen they would enter the school for greater learning, where henceforth their instruction was in principle, that is, in the extension of knowledge and the investigation of things as well as in what constitutes loyalty, trustworthiness, filiality, and fraternal respect. (7.124)

3.   Lesser learning is the study of affairs. Greater learning is the study of the reasons behind the affairs studied in lesser learning. (7.124)

4.   Lesser learning is about affairs, like serving one's ruler, serving one's father, serving one's elder brother, and dealing with one's friends. It simply teaches us to behave according to certain norms. Greater learning is about illuminating the principle behind these affairs. (7.125)

5.   The other night, Qiyuan[2] said that reverential attentiveness was no match for lesser learning. When I look at it, lesser learning is no match for reverential attentiveness. Reverential attentiveness already embodies lesser learning. Reverential attentiveness is to make the right effort everywhere. And even when one has entered the realm of the sages, this reverential attentiveness cannot be dispensed with. For instance, Yao and Shun were reverentially attentive from beginning to end. When

in celebrating Yao's virtue it is said that he was "reverent [*qin* 欽)] intelligent, accomplished, thoughtful,"[3] these four words put "being *jing*" [reverentially attentive] at the head of the list. And when it is said, "Assuming a reverential [*gong* 恭] pose, he [Shun] faced due south"[4] and "if he is sincere and reverent (*gong*), all under heaven will be at peace,"[5] it's the same.[6] (7.126)

6. In antiquity, lesser learning disciplined and trained people without their even knowing it. So when they grew up, they already naturally possessed a template for being a sage or worthy and would just add embellishments to it. Today, we have altogether abandoned efforts at lesser learning. Only if we instruct people to take reverential attentiveness as their master and to discipline their mind-hearts can they make the proper effort. Zhu added: Lesser learning of the ancients instructed people in affairs. As a matter of course their mind-hearts would be nurtured and, without realizing it, they would naturally become good. With time and experience they would come to comprehend affairs and things—until there was nothing they could not do. People today have no foundation and attend to useless matters, doing this and thinking about that. Conversely, they do harm to their mind-hearts. (7.125)

7.   Lu Zishou[7] said: In antiquity, young children, as soon as they were able to talk and eat, were instructed in matters like cleaning and sweeping and polite conversation. And they would practice them. Consequently, when they grew up, they could converse easily with others. These days people at an early age are taught to compose couplets and a little later they are taught to compose showy prose, all of which spoils their original nature. I have thought about developing a set of regulations for lesser learning so that early on people might be educated according to a plan. Something like this would surely be beneficial.

The Master said: It would be good just to design something along the lines of the *Chanyuan Code* [*Chanyuan qinggui* 禪苑清規].[8] (7.126)

8.   Someone asked: Women too ought to receive instruction. In addition to the *Classic on Filial Piety*, how about selecting for instruction passages from the *Analects* that are straightforward and clear?

Zhu replied: Yes, that would be good. The Cao Family's *Lessons for Women* [*Nüjie* 女戒][9] and *Wengong's [Sima Guang's] Precepts for Family Life* [*Wengong jiafan* 溫公家範] would also be good. (7.127)

9.   Since heaven first gave birth to the people down below, it has granted them all the same nature of goodness, righteousness, propriety, and wisdom. Yet their endowments of psychophysical stuff often prove unequal; so not all are able to know the composition of their natures and thus to preserve them whole. Should there appear among the people one who is bright and wise, capable of fulfilling the capacity of his nature, heaven would certainly ordain him to act as sovereign and instructor to the multitudes, commissioning him to govern and teach them so that their natures be restored.

Thus, Fu Xi, Shen Nong, Huangdi, Yao, and Shun[10] carried on for heaven and established the highest point of excellence; and these were the reasons for which the office of the Minister of Education and the post of the Director of Music were founded.

Amidst the glory of the Three Dynasties,[11] regulations were gradually perfected, and thereafter schools were found everywhere, from the Imperial Palace and state capitals on down to the villages. At age eight all the male children, from the sons of kings and dukes to the sons of commoners, entered the school of lesser learning; there they were instructed in the chores of cleaning and sweeping, in the formalities of polite conversation and good manners, and in the refinements of ritual, music, archery, charioteering, calligraphy, and mathematics. At age fifteen, the Son of Heaven's eldest son and other imperial sons on down to the eldest legitimate sons of dukes, ministers, high officials, and officers of the chief grade, together with the gifted from among the populace, all entered the school of greater learning; there they were instructed in the Way of probing principle, setting the mind-heart in the right, cultivating oneself and governing others. This was the way instruction in the schools was divided into programs of greater and lesser learning.

Such was the scope of the establishment of schools; such too were the details of the sequence and program of instruction. As for the content of the instruction, it was based entirely on principles drawn from the sovereign's personal experience and deep understanding, and yet it consisted of nothing more than the standards of right conduct to be followed by the people in their daily lives. Thus all in that age advanced in learning, and, in their advancement, they all came to know the primal constitution of their natures, and at the same time, the duties that were demanded of each of them. Each person was diligent and put forth his utmost effort. This is why in the heyday of antiquity good government flourished above and excellent customs prevailed bellow—it was a period never equaled by later generations.

As the Zhou declined, worthy and sage sovereigns did not arise, administration of schools was not kept up, education deteriorated, mores degenerated. Though a Sage like Confucius appeared in such times, he did not attain the position of sovereign-instructor, the position from which he could enact his policies and teachings. Alone, he took the ways of the former kings, recited and passed them on to his disciples, to proclaim them to later generations. . . .

With the death of Mencius the transmission ceased, and though the text [of the *Greater Learning*] was preserved, there were few who understood it. From then on, vulgar Confucians devoted twice as much effort to memorization and recitation, and to the composition of ornate verse and essays as they did to lesser learning, yet what they achieved was of no use. The heterodox teachings of emptiness and inaction, of calmness and extinction seemed "loftier" than greater learning yet they were without application to the real world. In addition, there appeared all manner of intrigues and stratagems—that is counsels designed to lead to great success and fame—together with sects of the "hundred schools" and the "multitudinous experts," which confuse the world, deceive the people, and obstruct the path of true goodness and righteousness. These caused the ruler, unable to hear the essentials of the Great Way, misfortune; these caused the common people misfortune, unable to enjoy the best government. Like a chronic disease, gloom and obstruction persisted, until decay and chaos reached their peak with the end of the Five Dynasties.[12]

Heaven moves in cycles: nothing goes that does not come back to its origins. So the virtuous force of the Song appeared in all its glory, and instruction flourished. At this time, the two Cheng brothers of Henan appeared, and found it within their capacity to take up again the tradition of Mencius. Indeed, they were the first to give due honor to the *Greater Learning* and to make it known to the world; and, after putting the text in order, they explicated its essential points. Only then was the system of teaching employed in the school for greater learning in antiquity— the subject of the Sage's *Classics* and worthies' commentary— brilliantly illuminated for the world again. Though I acknowledge my ignorance, I was still fortunate to have learned indirectly [from the Cheng brothers], so share in having heard the tradition.[13]

B. LEARNING, THE GENERAL PRINCIPLES

10. The substance of the Way is infinite. (8.129)

11. Although the substance and operation of the Way are subtle in the extreme, the explanations of the sages and worthies are very clear. (8.129)

12. In the teaching of others, the sages mostly talked about filiality, brotherly respect, loyalty and trustworthiness, and everyday routine behavior. If people are able to put these teachings into practice, their lost mind-hearts will naturally be recovered and their obscured human nature will naturally become manifest. "Mind-heart," "human nature," and other words were first discussed in detail by Zisi 子思[14] and Mencius. (8.129)

13. The everyday effort required by the Confucian school appears to be extremely simple, and yet the principle derived from it is all-embracing and all-penetrating. Extend it and it will be as vast as heaven and earth. For this reason, to be a sage, to be a worthy, to put heaven and earth in their proper order, and to nourish the myriad things, are all matters of this one principle and nothing more. (8.130)

14. The learning of the ordinary people often inclines toward one manifestation of principle alone and focuses on just one idea; and as a consequence, they don't see all four sides. This leads to quarrels with others. The sage is balanced and harmonious and does not lean one way or another. (8.130)

15. What all the sages and worthies say about making the proper effort is similar. It is just "to choose the good and firmly hold fast to it."[15] In the *Analects*, it is said, "To learn and rehearse it constantly,"[16] and in the *Mencius* it is said, "Understand the good and make oneself authentic."[17] Because each speaks from its own point of view, what they literally say is different. But put the words aside and consider each passage in detail and, in fact, the proper effort they call for is similar. Only when you appreciate why the texts are different will you understand that what they say is the same. (8.130)

16. I worry that in their practice students will not get the essentials. If they investigate the principle of the Way, everything naturally will fall into place, interconnecting with everything else, and each thing in proper sequence. But if they don't, they'll run into difficulties everywhere. Students talk nonstop,

speaking frequently of "holding on to it," but if they haven't yet understood the essentials, they don't know what "to hold on to." They talk of "extending it" or "personally experiencing it" or "nurturing it"—all are instances of choosing the right words for conversation's sake. But only when they are truly capable of these things is it okay. When it is said, "focus on the essentials," it's likely for this reason. (8.130)

17. In learning, first establish the framework and then turn to the interior to put up walls and corners. This will make for a well-constructed edifice. People today frequently proceed directly to building half of a one-room house even before they're familiar with the general plans. As a consequence, what they have done is of little use. (8.130)

18. The sages and worthies simply did to the fullest what a person ought to do. To become a sage or worthy today just stop right there and go no further. (8.133)

19. In learning, you'll start benefiting only once you've made the "big advance." If you're able to penetrate the one big point [i.e., the principle of the Way], you'll take pleasure in realizing that the various smaller fragments are just this one principle of the Way. It's not that you shouldn't give attention to the smaller fragments. But if you have yet to penetrate the big point, though you might pay attention to a few of the smaller fragments, you'll take no pleasure in it. Zeng Dian and Qidiao Kai* knew what their big hopes were simply because they had come to appreciate the big point. Now, let's talk about what that big thing is: under heaven there is just the one principle of the Way. In learning you want simply to understand this one principle of the Way. Once this is understood completely, heavenly principle and human desires, righteousness and profit, impartiality and partiality will all be completely understood. (8.131)

---

*Disciples of Confucius in the *Analects*.

20. Complete yourself and only then will you be able to complete other things. The completion of things lies in the completion of the self. Only if you extend outward from the self like this will you be able to accord with moral principle. The myriad words of the sages and worthies teach people to proceed from what is near-at-hand. For instance, sprinkling and sweeping the main hall is just like sprinkling and sweeping a small room. Once you've swept clean a small place, a large place is no different. If you can't clear the land in a large area, it's because you have never fully exerted yourself in a small area. Students are fond of the lofty and the remote and are unwilling to proceed from what is near-at-hand. How can they possibly understand large matters? Today there are those who don't proceed from within and yet outwardly do quite well. This is simply because they are enormously talented and the power of their intellect triumphs. The *Mean* says of the minute: be watchful in your solitude, watchful in your words, watchful in your actions.[18] Of the large it says, King Wen and the Duke of Zhou were far-reaching in their filial piety; and they regulated everything under heaven without exception.[19] The small leads to the fulfilment of the large; you must strive to be watchful in your actions and watchful in your words, and only then will you be capable of bringing the large to completion, as they did. (8.131)

21. The difference between the ordinary sort of learning and that of the sages and worthies is really not hard to see. Sages and worthies are truly intent on action. When they talk about "setting the mind-heart in the right," they truly want to set the mind-heart in the right; and when they talk about "making the intentions true," they truly want to make the intentions true. Nor are "cultivation of the self" and "bringing harmony to the household" just empty words for them.[20] When students today talk about setting the mind-heart in the right, they're but briefly mouthing the words "setting the mind-heart in the right;" and when they

talk about making the intentions true, they're but briefly mouthing the words "making the intentions true." And when they talk about cultivation of the self, they're just reciting the various explanations of self-cultivation by the sages and worthies and nothing more. At times they gather up the words of the sages and worthies and compose examination essays. This sort of learning has no effect on their own persons. You must be intent on understanding this. Our friends today, to be sure, take pleasure in the learning of the sages and worthies, but in the end they are incapable of breaking away from the ordinary practices of the day. It's simply that their wills are not fixed and nothing more. Establishing the will is of greatest importance to students. The moment they begin their learning, they should be set on becoming sages. (8.133)

22. Today it's important to understand what makes a sage and what makes an ordinary person, and why we are not like the sages but are merely ordinary people. When we understand this fully, we can naturally transcend the common and enter into sagehood. (8.134)

23. In studying, it's critical to consider how to transcend the common and enter sagehood—how we can be an ordinary villager yesterday and today become a sage! We must raise ourselves up and only then will we start to make progress. (8.135)

24. Students today are not the least bit zealous. (8.135)

25. Don't wait! (8.135)

26. People today are slow to commence their efforts at learning—they all prefer to wait. If they're busy this morning and not this afternoon, they could get started this afternoon, and if they're busy this afternoon, they could get started this evening. But they are sure to want to wait until tomorrow. And if there are still a few days left in this this month, they are certain simply to wait until next month; if there are a few months left in this year, they will not make the effort, and are sure to say, "There

isn't much time remaining this year, we should wait until next year." How are they going to make any progress behaving like this? (8.135)

27. Generally, in learning, though a person might have the natural gift of intelligence, only if he makes the effort of a dullard will he begin to understand. A person with the natural disposition of a dullard, even if he makes the effort of an intelligent person, can't possibly understand! (8.136)

28. In learning, do not claim that there is no one to analyze it for you. Make the right effort, examining into the core of it yourself. You must understand it for yourself. (8.136)

29. You cannot depend on teachers and friends. (8.135)

30. Make your curriculum small but your effort on it large. (8.136)

31. Just understand it—no need to calculate the gain you will get from it. (8.136)

32. As soon as you calculate the gain, your mind-heart will divide in two and your head will hang. (8.136)

33. Establish a strict work schedule, relax your thoughts, and after a while you should naturally get the meaning. You must not look for quick results. (8.136)

34. From morning 'til evening there is no time when we needn't make purposeful effort. (8.136)

35. Zonggao[21] said: "If you had a cartload of military weapons and grabbed one at a time, tinkering first with this one and then with that one—this would be no way to kill someone. Yet, if I had nothing but a short dagger, I could kill someone!" (8.137)

36. In learning, grab hold of the boat-pole with all your strength. As you sense your effort beginning to flag, intensify it, applying all of your strength without letup, and only then will you make progress. Learning is exactly like punting a boat upstream: Only in calm spots does the boat move along without hindrances. When it enters the rapids, the boatman takes up his

pole and doesn't let go of it. He must punt the boat upstream with all of his strength, without relaxing for a moment. If he lightens up for a moment this boat won't make it upstream. (8.137)

37. Managing the myriad affairs successfully requires the presence of one's vital spirit [*jingshen* 精神]. (8.138)

38. When yang psychophysical stuff issues forth, even metal and stone can be penetrated. And as soon as the vital spirit arrives anything can be accomplished. (8.138)

39. A person's psychophysical stuff must be hard if he is to manage affairs successfully. Consider: the psychophysical stuff of heaven and earth is hard and, as a result, it can penetrate every single thing and affair. The hardness of people's psychophysical stuff is essentially like this as well. But if a person backs off when encountering a thing or affair, however trivial or important, what can he accomplish? (8.138)

40. Students today are simply not learning for their own sake and, thus, in the course of a day their mind-heart is rarely occupied with moral principle and often occupied with trivial matters. They remain unfamiliar with moral principle even as their familiarity with the trivial grows deeper. (8.139)

41. It's important that today's students distinguish between the paths. What's important is the boundary between "doing it for the sake of yourself" and "doing it for the sake of others." Doing it for the sake of yourself is to acquire a firsthand understanding of things and affairs—it's to want to understand them for yourself. It's not to understand them recklessly or to understand them in a way that makes you look good and invites others to remark on your understanding of them. And supposing you did understand them 100 percent accurately, that understanding would still have no effect on you at all. It's crucial that you first understand these paths. Only once you distinguish clearly between them, can you understand the texts. (8.139)

42. In recent times, scholarly discussion hasn't been genuine. Typically, people just want to show off. It can be compared to someone who has food, but, rather than eating it himself, sets it outside his gates so that others will know his family has food. Only when such thinking is fully reformed will there be progress. (8.139)

43. As it is, people today are mostly negligent in their learning. They're never truly willing to do it. (8.139)

44. Learning must genuinely be for one's own sake. If it is, one will become tranquil and true and embody the various manifestations of the principle of the Way. If a person's learning is but superficial, how's he going to investigate moral principle? And supposing he were to investigate it, and then explain it to others, he still would not embody it. (8.140)

45. To enter the gates of the Way, immerse yourself in the principle of the Way. You'll gradually become intimately familiar with it, and over time become one with it. But with people today, the principle of the Way is here, and they themselves remain there, external to it, and have nothing to do with it. (8.140)

46. It's best if you yourself see your shortcomings, but that others see the progress you've made. (8.142)

47. "Extensive learning"[22] refers to all that we ought to learn: the principle of heaven, earth, and the myriad things and the way to cultivate the self and govern others. Still, there's an order to it all. It's appropriate that the big and the urgent come first. Don't be unsystematic or piecemeal. (8.142)

48. If we liken it [learning] to climbing a mountain, people mostly want to get to the highest points, not realizing that unless they're familiar with the lower points there will be no getting to the higher ones! (8.142)

49. What I fear most is reading carelessly and easily falling into no good. (8.143)

50. If you just hold a piece of fruit in your hand, you won't know whether its inside is acidic or salty, bitter or harsh. You have to bite into it to appreciate its flavor. (8.145)

51. If we ourselves don't feel good about our own ideas, how could others possibly feel good about them! It's important to "open" our mind-hearts and follow goodness. (8.145)

52. "Open your mind-heart and accord with principle" [*xuxin shunli* 虛心順理]. Students should abide by this four-character phrase. (8.145)

53. People these days say that in talking about the principle of the Way they aim to be simple, but don't realize that to be simple in this matter is extremely difficult. Entangled in old habits, how are we to shake free of them? It's like writing: composing something novel and artful is easy, but if your aim is to be simple and plain, that is hard. Only after you've rejected the novel and artful will you advance to the simple and plain. He added: To move down from a high and precipitous spot to a level and clear one is extremely challenging. (8.145)

54. I have only heard the phrase "my studies lie low, and so my penetration rises high."[23] I have never heard the phrase "my penetration rises high, and so my studies lie low." (8.146).

55. Only if you engage in learning on the lower level will you be capable of penetration on the higher level. Still, there are people who engage in learning on the lower level and are incapable of penetration on the higher level. This is simply because their learning on the lower level is inadequate. If it were adequate, they would be capable of penetration on the higher level. The Buddhists speak only of penetration on the higher level and give little attention to learning on the lower level. But giving little attention to learning on the lower level, how are they to achieve penetration on the higher level? (44.1140)

56. The virtue of teachers and friends is simply that at the start they can show you what learning is and at the end correct

what you have learned. The middle 30 percent requires vigorous effort on your own part. Having received instruction at the start and labored on your own in the middle, you can then confer with others and correct what you have learned—and the benefits will be great. If you don't proceed like this, it will be of no help to you. (8.146)

57. It's urgent that you do away with the mind-heart that clings to externals. (8.147)

58. Once you intimately understand this principle of the Way, it alone will be your one true standard. You'll see the myriad affairs of the world as topsy-turvy and confused, dissolute and lustful, and all part of an elaborate play—you won't bear to look. He also wrote in response to someone: "The myriad affairs of the world transform and perish in a moment's time. You should not attach to them. Let probing principle and cultivating the self be your one true model." (8.147)

C. Extending Knowledge and Probing Principle[24]

59. To say the "extension of knowledge lies in the investigation of things" means that if we wish to extend our knowledge to the utmost, we must probe thoroughly the principle in those things we encounter. It would seem that every person's intellect is possessed of the capacity for knowing and that everything in the world is possessed of principle. But, to the extent that principle is not yet thoroughly probed, a person's knowledge is not yet fully realized. Hence, the first step of instruction in greater learning is to teach the student, whenever he encounters anything at all in the world, to build on what is already known to him of principle and to probe still further, seeking to reach the limit. After exerting himself in this way for a long time, he will one day become enlightened and understand thoroughly; then, the manifest and the hidden, and the subtle and obvious qualities

of all things will all be known, and the mind-heart, in its whole substance and vast operations, will be completely illuminated. This is called "things having been investigated." This is called "the perfection of knowledge."[25]

60. Typically, knowledge and action are both necessary. If you have eyes but no feet you will not walk; if you have feet and no eyes you will not see. If we speak of their sequence, knowledge comes first; if we speak of their importance, action is more important. (9.148)

61. There was discussion of the relationship between knowledge and action, and Zhu said: When you know it but don't practice it, your knowledge is still superficial. Once you've personally experienced it, your knowledge of it will be much clearer and its significance will be different from what it had been previously. (9.148)

62. In "extending knowledge to the utmost"[26] and "acting vigorously"[27] do not let your effort be one-sided. If it inclines too much toward one, the other will suffer. As Master Cheng said, "Nurturing requires reverential attentiveness, and the pursuit of learning depends on the extension of knowledge."[28] Clearly his ideas rested on two legs, but it's important to distinguish their relative sequence and importance. To speak of their sequence, it's proper to place the extension of knowledge first; to speak of their importance, it's proper to give more weight to vigorous action. (9.148)

63. There simply exist two matters: understanding and practice. (9.149)

64. What we mean by "probing principle" is that the big is to be probed and the small is to be probed and soon they will all become one. What we mean by "keeping a fast hold on it" is that people can't but be enticed by creaturely desires, and only when they realize it, do they rein themselves in. Over time they will naturally become accustomed to it. It isn't that

today they all at once begin to feel accustomed to reining themselves in. (9.149)

65. Zizhi asked: If you nurture yourself, after a while will you naturally become enlightened?

Zhu said: You must also probe principle. Nurturing and probing principle are both indispensable, like the two wheels of a cart or the two wings of a bird. Take Wengong [Sima Guang] for instance: he only acted and ignored the extension of knowledge. (9.150)

66. Holding fast to reverential attentiveness is the basis of probing principle; and probing principle until it is clear, in turn, helps in nurturing the mind-heart. (9.150)

67. Students who don't probe principle won't come to understand the principle of the Way; but those who probe principle and don't hold fast to reverential attentiveness won't come to understand it either. If they don't hold fast to reverential attentiveness, the principle of the Way will appear completely diffuse and won't come together here in this one spot. (9.151)

68. Someone asked about the order of extending knowledge and nurturing the self.

Zhu replied: You must first extend knowledge and afterward nurture yourself.

Someone asked: What about Yichuan's [Cheng Yi's] saying, "It is impossible to extend knowledge without practicing reverential attentiveness."[29]

Zhu replied: Here he was speaking generally. If you want to probe principle you must give it your full attention. If you don't, how are you going to understand clearly? (9.152)

69. Wang Zichong asked: When I was in Hunan, I visited a teacher [likely Zhang Shi] who taught others only to act.

Zhu replied: If moral principle isn't clear how can we act?

Wang said: He said, "When you do it you understand it."

Zhu replied: This is like a person walking along a path. If he doesn't see, how is he going to walk the path. People today frequently instruct others to act. Having established this standard, they convey it to others in their teaching. Of course, there are those persons with naturally good constitutions who needn't probe principle, investigate things, or extend knowledge. But the Sage wrote the *Greater Learning* so that all people can enter the realm of sages and worthies. Once they understand the principle of the Way, in serving parents they're sure to be filial, in serving brothers they're sure to be fraternal, and in dealing with friends they're sure to be trustworthy. (9.152)

70. In learning a person must aim to know with certainty what is right. When he knows through and through that this is right and through and through that this is wrong, his understanding will be thorough. And understanding what is right, his mind-heart will have its master. Suppose a person takes up archery: if he sets his mind-heart on the bull's eye, soon he'll occasionally hit the target. If he sets his mind-heart on the target, soon he'll occasionally hit the target-mound. If he sets his mind-heart on the target-mound, soon he'll routinely hit some other place altogether. (9.154)

71. It's merely a struggle between knowing and not knowing, and between knowing it well and not well. Let's say someone wants to do the good thing but then happens to see the bad and seems capable of doing it as well. Just as he's about to do the good thing, it's as though the mind-heart to do the bad comes from behind and leads him astray. This is simply to "not know it well." (9.154)

72. Humans, heaven, and earth all possess manifestations of the principle of the Way. It is not that we force principles on them or cut open their bowels and place them there. (9.154)

73. The one mind-heart embodies the myriad manifestation of principle. If you're capable of preserving the mind-heart, you then can probe principle. (9.154)

74. The mind-heart embraces the myriad manifestations of principle. The myriad manifestations of principle are embodied in the one mind-heart. To be incapable of preserving the mind-heart is to be incapable of probing principle and to be incapable of probing principle is to be incapable of fully realizing the mind-heart. (9.155)

75. To probe principle, an open mind-heart [*xuxin*] and quiet reflection are essential. (9.155)

76. Open your mind-heart [*xuxin*] to observe principle. (9.155)

77. If today we look for the principle of the Way but fail to see it, it isn't that we do not recognize it, it's simply that it is obstructed by things. The common way to deal with this is to dispose of the evil distractions in the mind—and then we'll see it. Master Zhang said, "If moral principle is obstructed,[30] wash away your old understanding and bring forth new ideas." Mostly, people are attached to their old understandings and unwilling to give them up—except for especially intelligent ones who see what isn't right and disavow it. (9.155)

78. Principle isn't some distinct thing in front of us; it's in our mind-hearts. People must discover for themselves that this thing is truly within them, then everything will be okay. It's similar to what the school of inner cultivation [inner alchemical Daoists] calls "lead and mercury, dragon and tiger." They are things within us, not outside of us. (9.155)

79. Qiyuan asked: In probing principle in things and affairs, should we be searching for a point of convergence, or what?

Zhu replied: No need to talk of convergence. All that appears before our eyes are affairs and things. Just probe each and every one to its limit and gradually the many, on their own, will become interconnected. Where they converge is in the mind-heart. (9.155)

80. Once you come to understand the principle of the Way, you will be in accord with what ought to be. Take the case of a

bamboo chair: it has to have four legs to be level and upright, and only then can you sit in it. If it is without a leg, you absolutely can't sit in it. If you don't understand this and assume that two or three legs are fine, when you go to sit on it, it simply won't work. Putting a ring in the nose of a cow or a halter around the head of a horse merely conforms to the norms of heavenly principle. If you were to put a ring in the horse's nose and halter around the cow's head, it certainly would not do. We were just now explaining "subduing the self,"[31] which Yichuan had simply explained as being reverentially attentive. People today likewise know to be reverentially attentive, but they don't routinely hold to it. If they did, in little time they would understand right from wrong and the principle of the Way clearly. (9.156)

81. Moral principle is infinite. What our predecessors have said about it isn't necessarily exhaustive. We must pick it up ourselves and look at it from every angle, penetrating it deeply and immersing ourselves in it. (9.157)

82. Students today do not have intimate understanding. Rather they conjecture and speculate—defects of "helping it grow."[†] Just observe the principle of the Way calmly and its meaning will naturally become evident. Don't have preconceived notions about it. (9.158)

83. Seeing the meaning in a text is difficult. You need to relax your mind-heart and, at the same time, concentrate it. When this mind-heart is not relaxed it is incapable of grasping the general sweep of the text; and when it's not concentrated it is incapable of examining the thread of the argument in detail. And should

---

†*Mencius* 2A.2. A man from Song pulled at the sprouts in his field hoping to help them grow. Instead, they shriveled up and died. This is the defect of "helping it grow." Likewise, conjecturing and speculating do injury to the true principle of the Way.

it get stuck on the meaning of words, soon it won't understand the general sweep of the text. (9.158)

84. Rely on the thoughts of the sages and worthies when looking at the books of the sages and worthies; rely on the principle of all under heaven when looking at the affairs of all under heaven. In probing principle people mostly rely on their personal understanding, and their understanding is still quite a remove from the mind-heart of the sages and worthies. (9.159)

85. Rumination is like digging a well—don't stop and you'll hit clear water. It's sure to be muddy at first; but dredge it little by little and it will naturally become clear. (9.159)

86. In knowing there is simply a distinction between the true and the untrue. To say there is a knowing that is ineffable is the fallacy of the Buddhists. (9.159.)

87. Those who are dedicated to seeking it within regard broad investigation as rushing toward the external, while those dedicated to broad investigation regard self-examination as constricting and falling into one-sidedness. Both these practices are serious defects in students. (9.160)

The goal of learning is to apprehend the principle that underlies the universe and gives coherence to it. By apprehending principle, we can come to appreciate the order of the universe and help to maintain it by playing our role in it. Principle, as we now know, resides in each and every thing. To apprehend it, then, students theoretically could turn anywhere—looking for principle in a hut, a tree, a bamboo grove, a father-son relationship, or an affair of state.

This could become unwieldy. Zhu Xi thus narrowed the field of study, hoping to make the investigation of principle more efficient and systematic. Students should focus their efforts on reading. Not just any texts, of course, but the Confucian Classics, the writings of the sages and worthies. Because these sages and worthies fully embodied and manifested principle in their lives, Zhu was convinced that their written words manifested principle more readily and clearly than anywhere else. In short, accessing principle in a great Classic would be easier, Zhu thought, than accessing it, for instance, through the investigation of a willow tree.

But the canon was not to be read in some random order. Because of their relative "ease, immediacy, and brevity,"[1] students should begin with the Four Books—the *Greater Learning*, the *Analects*, the *Mencius*, and the *Mean*. For him, these texts constituted the core curriculum, the ones to be read before all others by those pursuing the Confucian Way. In 1190, Zhu published these texts together in a collection for the first time; they would quickly come to displace the Five Classics—the *Book of Changes*, the *Classic of Odes*, the *Classic of History*, the *Book of Rites*, and the *Spring and Autumn Annals*—as the authoritative, core texts in the Confucian tradition. Students, of course, were still expected to turn to the Five Classics, but only after mastering the Four Books.

In favoring a sequenced curriculum, Zhu went still further, prescribing a standard order in which the Four Books themselves are to be read. "In learning you must start with the *Greater Learning*, next read the *Analects*, next read the *Mencius*, next the *Mean*" (14.249), he told his students. And it is this order that ever since has been enshrined in the tradition.

Having read the Four Books and Five Classics, students will have internalized "the standard of measure," Zhu claimed, and can then move on to the standard historical works like the *Records of the Grand Historian*, the *Zuo Commentary on the Spring and Autumn Annals*, the *Comprehensive Mirror for Aid in Government*, and the dynastic histories. The Classics will have provided them with a "measuring stick" to judge fairly historical events and personages and to draw the right lessons from China's past.

So critical was effective reading to Zhu Xi's program of moral cultivation that he not only devoted considerable attention to the curriculum of texts but he also laid out in great detail how texts should be read. In fact, his comments on how to read—what Zhu and editor Li Jingde called *dushufa* (讀書法, literally "method of reading")—fill two chapters of the *Zhuzi yulei* (*Classified Conversations*, chapters 10 and 11). Students were not merely to read the texts, they were to "experience" them and "make them their own." For Zhu, the canonical writings were the medium for transmitting the mind of the sages and worthies of antiquity to the Song reader's mind. As Zhu put it in one exchange with pupils: "In reading, we first need to become familiar with the text so that its words all seem to come from our own mouths. We should continue to reflect on it so that its ideas come from our own mind-hearts" (10.168). The reader's mind is thus transformed and becomes one with the mind of the great sages.

A. Why Read

1. All things in the world have principle; the essence of principle is embodied in the works of the sages and worthies. Hence, in seeking principle we must turn to these works.[2]

2. Reading is of secondary importance. It would seem that the principle of the Way is originally complete in human beings. But because they don't experientially understand much, they have to read. The sages did experientially understand a great deal and so wrote it down for others to see. In reading today we just need to come to understand the many manifestations of the principle of the Way. When we do, we will find that all of them were complete within us from the very beginning, and not added on to us from the outside. (10.161)

3. Read in order to observe the intentions of the sages and worthies. Follow the intentions of the sages and worthies in order to observe natural principle. (10.162)

4. Open up a text and you'll see how you are different from the sages and worthies. Can you possibly not goad yourself on!? (10.162)

5. In learning, people should really aim to acquire it in their mind-hearts and embody it in their bodies. But if they do not read books, they will not appreciate what their mind-hearts are supposed to acquire. (11.176)

6. People who read constantly can pretty much control their own mind-heart and thereby keep it constantly preserved. Hengqu [Zhang Zai] had a saying: "Books are the way to maintain the mind-heart. The moment you put them down is the moment your virtue grows lax. Can you possibly abandon them?"[3] (11.176)

7. Beginning students are sure to have lapses in reverential attentiveness. It's only when they recognize the lapses that they

rouse their mind-hearts. And it's only with this recognition then that reverential attentiveness resumes. I hope that people, in reading, will grasp moral principle for themselves. If they read all day long their mind-hearts will not grow reckless. Yet sometimes they simply get caught up in the affairs and things of the world and their mind-hearts get easily submerged. If they know that this is the case, and in their reading grasp moral principle for themselves, they can summon a return of the mind-heart. (11.176)

8. When the original mind-heart has been submerged for a while and moral principle is drowning and impenetrable, it's fitting to read books and probe principle. Do this without interruption and the mind-heart of human desires will naturally be incapable of winning out and moral principle in the original mind-heart will be safe and secure. (11.176)

9. Only when preserving the mind-heart and reading books constitute one matter will you get it. (11.177)

10. People have self-centered ideas. The sages and worthies set down their myriad words in order to clear away these self-centered ideas and allow everyone to preserve whole their mind-hearts of compassion and shame. The Six Classics do not have an iota of self-centeredness in them.[4] (11.188)

B. WHAT TO READ

THE CONFUCIAN CLASSICS

11. The sages wrote the Classics in order to teach later generations. These texts enable readers to reflect on the ideas of the sages while reciting their words and hence to understand what is in accordance with the principle of things. Understanding the whole substance of the proper Way, they will practice the Way

with all their strength, and so enter the realm of the sages and worthies. Although the texts are concise, they treat all matters under heaven, the hidden and the manifest, the great and the small. If they who wish to seek the Way and thereby enter into virtue abandon the Classics, they will have nothing to which to apply themselves.[5]

12. Best to read the texts of the sages. Understanding their ideas is just like speaking with them face to face. (10.162)

13. Because we have commentary on the Classics, we understand the Classics. Once we have understood the Classics there is naturally no need for commentary. We depend on the Classics simply to understand principle. And when principle is understood there is no need for the Classics. If today our thoughts are bogged down in these texts, when will they become free to understand principle? (11.192)

14. Of the commentaries, only the ancient ones are not independent essays and good to read. They explain each line of classical text, never parting from its meaning. This is best. The subcommentaries are the same. In annotating texts today, people want to write independent essays, presenting their own arguments and raising all sorts of questions. What they write may be readable, but they stray far from the meaning of the Classics. Master Cheng's *Commentary on the Changes* is just such an independent essay, discussing this and that. Thus, when people today read it, they don't look at the original Classic but only at the *Commentary*, which doesn't allow them to think about the Classic itself. (11.193)

15. The texts of the sages' Classics are like the master, the commentaries like the slave. Nowadays, people are unacquainted with the master and turn to the slave for an introduction to him. Only in this way do they become acquainted with the master, which in the end can't compare to turning directly to the texts of the Classics. (11.193)

THE FOUR BOOKS AS THE CORE CURRICULUM

16. The first thing our Masters Cheng from Henan taught others was to apply themselves to the *Greater Learning*, the *Analects*, the *Mean*, and the *Mencius*. Afterward they were to turn to the Six Classics.[6]

17. The *Greater Learning* provides the outline for learning. Come first to a full understanding of the *Greater Learning* to determine the general principia of learning; the other Classics are all explained therein. Once you have thoroughly understood the *Greater Learning*, turn to the other Classics and you'll appreciate what it means to "apprehend the principle in things" and extend knowledge to the utmost"; what it means to "set the mind-heart in the right" and "make the intentions true"; what it means to "cultivate the self"; and what it means to "establish harmony in the household," "govern the state well," and "bring tranquility to the empire." (14.252)

18. If we wish principle to be simple and easy to appreciate, concise and easy to grasp, there is nothing better than the *Greater Learning*, the *Analects*, the *Mencius*, and the *Mean*.[7]

19. In reading, begin with passages that are easy to understand. For example, principle is brilliantly clear in the *Greater Learning*, the *Mean*, the *Analects*, and the *Mencius*, these four texts. Men simply do not read them. If these texts were understood, any book could be read, any principle could be investigated, any affair could be managed. (14.249)

20. Beginning students must read the *Greater Learning*, the *Analects*, and the *Mencius*. If they study the *Greater Learning* thoroughly, they will understand the other texts without much effort. He sighed for a while, then said: There is indeed such a principle, but when I explain it to others, they don't believe it. (19.440)

21. The *Analects* and the *Mencius* are the most important works for the student pursuing the Way. . . . The words of the *Analects*

are all-inclusive; what they teach is nothing but the essentials of preserving the mind-heart and cultivating the nature. The main points of the seven books [of the *Mencius*] are all-probing; what they teach mostly is the realization and development of the originally good nature. Such indeed is the difference between the Sage and the Worthy. Yet substance and function have a single source, and the manifest and the hidden are indivisible.[8]

Reading the Four Books Sequentially

22. In learning you must start with the *Greater Learning*; next read the *Analects*, next the *Mencius*, next the *Mean*. (14.249)

23. It would seem that if one does not read the *Greater Learning* first there is no way to grasp the outline of learning and thereby appreciate fully the subtleties of the *Analects* and the *Mencius*. If one does not then read the *Greater Learning* with the *Analects* and the *Mencius*, there is no way to understand thoroughly the thread that runs through the three texts, and thereby to get at the essence of the *Mean*. Still, if one is not versed in the perfection expressed in the *Mean* how can one establish the great foundation or adjust the great invariable relations of man, how can one read the world's books or discuss the world's affairs? From this point of view it is apparent that those who engage in scholarly study must treat the Four Books with some urgency and those who study the Four Books must begin with the *Greater Learning*.[9]

24. I want men first to read the *Greater Learning* to fix upon the pattern of the Confucian Way; next the *Analects* to establish its foundations; next the *Mencius* to observe its development; next the *Mean* to discover the subtle mysteries of the ancients. The *Greater Learning* provides within its covers a series of steps and a precise order in which they should be followed; it is easy to understand and so should be read first. Although the *Analects* is

concrete, its sayings are scattered about in fragments; on first reading it is difficult. The *Mencius* contains passages that inspire and arouse men's mind-hearts. The *Mean*, too, is difficult to understand and should be read only after the other three books. (14.249)

25. Focus on the *Greater Learning*; when you have penetrated it thoroughly and have no questions, you can then read the *Analects* and the *Mencius*. When you have no questions about the *Analects* and the *Mencius*, you can then read the *Mean*. Now you do not fully understand the *Greater Learning* and yet at the same time you are also reading the *Mean*; you are giving your attention to too many matters. How can you expect to understand the texts in detail?[10]

26. The *Analects*, the *Mencius*, and the *Mean* should be read only after the *Greater Learning* has been thoroughly understood and no further reading seems necessary. The learning of the Way is unillumined to you, not principally because your effort on the higher level is deficient, but rather because you have no foothold on the lower level. If you were to get at the true meaning of the *Greater Learning*, thereby planting your feet on solid ground, your "true mind-heart" (*liangxin* 良心)[11] naturally would never be lost and your conduct naturally would be completely appropriate. (14.250)

27. Someone asked: I wish to focus on one text. Which should I start with?

Zhu replied: First read the *Greater Learning* so that you can see the order in which the ancients pursued learning. (14.250)

28. Yafu asked about the general import of the *Greater Learning*.

Zhu replied: The *Greater Learning* is the pattern for cultivating the self and governing others. It may be compared to a man building a house. He must first prepare the foundations; when the foundations have been completed, he may begin to build the house. (14.250)

29. People today learn for the sake of others. That's why I have you all read the *Greater Learning*. You will see how the ancients pursued learning and what their learning covered. Do you, sirs, want to engage in the sort of learning pursued by the ancients or the sort of learning pursued by your contemporaries? (14.253)

READING THE HISTORIES

30. Reading the Classics is different from reading the histories. The histories are secondary things, and not critical; we can take notes on them and raise our questions with others. But when we have doubts about the Classics, the anguish we feel is keen. We're like someone who is in physical pain and wants relief but can't get it. It's nothing like reading the histories. When doubts arise we can't just jot them down on a slip of paper! (11.189)

31. People nowadays have yet to read much in the Classics or thoroughly understand moral principle before they begin reading historical texts, inquiring into the order and disorder of the past and present, and studying institutions and the laws. This can be compared to building a dike to irrigate the fields: a dike should be full of water before you open it, then the water will rush out, nourishing all the crops in the field; if you hastily open the dike to irrigate the field just when the dike has accumulated little more than a ladleful of water, not only will this be of no benefit to the field, but you'll no longer have even the ladleful of water. Once you have read a lot in the Classics and you have thoroughly understood moral principle, your mind-heart will be completely clear as to the standard of measure; if you don't then turn to the historical texts, inquiring into the order and disorder of the past and present, and studying institutions and the laws, it's like having a dike full of water and not opening it to irrigate the field. If you have yet to read much in the Classics or thoroughly understand moral principles but eagerly make

reading the histories your first order of business, it's like open-ing a dike with a ladleful of water to irrigate the field. You can stand there and watch [the water] dry up. (11.195)

32. First read the *Analects*, the *Mencius*, and the *Mean*. Then read one of the [Five] Classics. Then read the histories, which at that point will be easy to read. Read the *Records of the Grand Historian* first. Since the *Records of the Grand Historian* and the *Zuo Commentary* cover much the same ground, next read the *Zuo Commentary*; next read the *Comprehensive Mirror for Aid in Government*, and, if you have strength remaining, read all the dynastic histories. Simply reading through the histories is not so good as reading through the twists and turns in them with an eye to the present. Observe that this is what order and disorder are, this is what victory and defeat are, and that "following the path of orderly government is certain to lead to prosperity, while following the path of disorder is certain to lead to ruin,"[12] and you'll appreciate the sequence of things. (11.195)

33. Today people don't read the classical texts; they read only the vulgar texts. Generally, in reading, if you read the *Analects* and the *Mencius* first and afterward the histories, it will be like having a clear mirror here where beautiful and ugly can't be mis-taken. But if you turn to the histories before thoroughly master-ing the *Analects*, the *Mencius*, the *Mean*, and the *Greater Learn-ing*, your mind-heart will have no measuring stick and will frequently be misled. There's another type of person who doesn't read at all and says, "I already understand the principle of the Way and that such-and-such is the mind-heart of compassion, such-and-such is the mind-heart of shame, and such-and-such is the mind-heart of right and wrong. All of this is his personal view. It's similar to what's been happening recently at the ances-tral temple.[13] (11.195)

34. In reading history, you should look for the great ethical principles, the great opportunities, and the instances of great order and disorder, and great success and failure. (11.196)

35. Generally, in reading the Classics and histories, focus on the right and the wrong. As you read the right, look for the wrong and, as you read the wrong, look for the right. Afterward you'll understand moral principle. (11.196)

36. In reading historical works, people must memorize certain parts to understand them. For instance, when reading the *Han History*, they should memorize the passage where Gaozu declines the Lordship of Pei, the one where Emperor Yi sends the Lord of Pei [i.e., Liu Bang] through the [Hangu] pass, the one where Han Xin for the first time persuades the King of Han [to head east], and other things like [Ban Gu's] historical eulogies [at the end of chapters in the *Han History*] and the "Faults of Qin."[14] If they merely race through the works, their mind-hearts will seem to get it at one moment and not at the next. That is of no use. In reading they must keep their mind-hearts on the text at all times to master it thoroughly from beginning to end: What is the meaning of this statement? What's the meaning of that statement? What are the agreements between the statements? What are the disagreements? Reading like this, how can they not make progress! (11.197)

C. How to Read

37. You should continually take the words of the sages and worthies and pass them before your eyes, roll them around and around in your mouth, and turn them over and over in your mind-heart. (10.162)

38. There is layer upon layer of meaning in the words of the sages. You must penetrate deeply in your reading. If you read only what's on the surface, you'll misunderstand. Only if you steep yourself in the words will you get the meaning. (10.162)

39. When students first read a text, they see it simply as a lump. In time they come to see it in two or three chunks, but it's

only when they come to see it in ten or more chunks that they'll make progress. It's like Cook Ding cutting up the ox—he got it just right when he no longer beheld the whole ox.[15] (10.163)

40. With each blow of the club let there be a scar; with each slap of the face let there be a handful of blood! Your reading of others' writings should be just like this. Don't be slack. (10.164)

41. In reading, relax the mind-heart and the principle of the Way will naturally appear. If you are anxious and feeling pressed, the principle of the Way has no way of appearing. (10.164)

42. Read less but become intimately familiar with what you read. Experience the text over and over. And do not think about gain. Hold to just these three matters at all times. (10.165)

43. Generally, in reading: (1) read little but become intimately familiar with what you read; (2) do not scrutinize a text looking to develop your own ideas about it, but simply experience it over and over; and (3) concentrate fully without thought of gain. Students ought to keep to these three dicta. (10.165)

44. In reading, keep the curriculum small and your effort on it large. If you are able to read two hundred characters, read only one hundred, but on those one hundred make a fierce effort. Come to understand them in detail, reciting them until they become intimately familiar to you. Read like this and those with weak memories will be able to remember and those with no comprehension will be able to understand. To read a lot, but carelessly, will be of no benefit. When you read a text, do not read it together with some other text you haven't read; read it together with texts you've read already. (10.165)

45. In reading, do not prize quantity; you just want to become intimately familiar with what you read. If today you can read one page, just read half a page, and then with the surplus strength read that same first half again. Do this with both halves and you'll come to understand the page intimately. And, it's best that you read for the meaning of the ancients. (10.166)

46. In your reading, just read one text at a time and each day read only one section of it. Only then will it begin to become your own. If you read around in this and that, though this and that will pass before your eyes, in the end you won't be intimately familiar with them. (10.166)

47. I especially don't want people to skip around when they read. They should understand each paragraph and each sentence. (10.167)

48. Reading is one way to investigate things. We must consider each paragraph of text carefully, over and over. If in one or two days we read through but one paragraph, this one paragraph will become our own. Once we have grasped the first paragraph, we can move on to the second. If we go on like this from paragraph to paragraph, we'll understand the principle of the Way through and through. The effort required of us involves constant thinking, whether we are in motion or at rest, sometimes taking what's already clear and turning it over in our minds a second and third time so that understanding emerges naturally. Even though the syntax and meaning of a text may have been explained to us, each time we read it will be a different experience. As a result, with certain texts each reading leads to a revised understanding. And where a text has already been explained definitively, each reading produces a sounder, and ever clearer, understanding. Therefore, I have said that in reading, do not value quantity, value only your familiarity with what you have read. This being the case, in your efforts advance boldly, without thought of retreating, and you'll begin to get it. (10.167)

49. People often race ahead and don't go back over earlier material. They just want to read tomorrow's still unread material; they don't bother to go back and examine what they read the previous day. But to begin to get it they must ponder over and over. Intense effort produces a far-reaching understanding;

and when understanding is far-reaching, benefits are assured. (10.167)

50. Generally, in reading you must read to the point of intimate familiarity. Intimate familiarity leads naturally to mastery, and with mastery, principle becomes evident of itself. It's similar to eating a piece of fruit. When you first bite into it you don't yet know the taste, and then you eat it. You must chew it thoroughly, and the taste will emerge naturally—and only then do you appreciate whether it is sweet or bitter and begin to know its taste. (10.167)

51. In my method of book learning it is essential to read diligently. Make a huge effort on the first book, and after that the effort need not be so great. At the outset, with the first book, the effort is total, with the next one it is 80 to 90 percent, and with the next one it is 40 to 50 percent. (10.167)

52. Generally speaking, in reading we first need to become intimately familiar with the text so that its words all seem to come from our own mouths. We should continue to reflect on it so that its ideas all seem to come from our own mind-hearts. Only then can we truly get it. If we are to make additional progress, that understanding—which arises from our intimate reading of it and reflection on it—must not mark the end of our questioning. If it does, there will never be further progress. (10.168)

53. If an ordinary person reads a book ten times and doesn't understand it, he should read it twenty times; if he still doesn't understand, he should read it thirty to fifty times, which is sure to yield some understanding. If after the fiftieth time, he is still unclear, it's because his psychophysical stuff is no good. People today don't read a book even ten times and then say they can't understand it. (10.168)

54. Do not keep a tally of the number of times you read a book. When the number is sufficient, stop. (10.169)

55. The value of a book is in the recitation of it alone. Frequent recitation results in understanding. If in thinking over a text you write it out on paper, it's of no real use, for in the end you haven't made the text your own. The value in a book is the recitation of it alone. I don't know why it is that the mind-heart naturally harmonizes with the psychophysical stuff, is uplifted and energized, and unfailingly remembers what it reads. Even supposing we were to read a book to the point of intimate familiarity and our mind-hearts were to ponder it, it wouldn't be as good as reciting it aloud. Recite it again and again and soon what's unclear will become clear, and what's already clear will become still more meaningful. (10.170)

56. The way to read is to read through the text, then ponder it; ponder it, then read it again. Recitation of it aids in the pondering by normally allowing the mind-heart to hover over the words. If it's simply the mouth doing the reciting and the mind-heart doing no pondering, what good is the reading? You'll remember nothing in detail. He further said: Because the number of printed texts nowadays is large, people don't apply their mind-hearts in reading them. In the Han period, transmission of the classics by scholars depended on recitation from memory. And so they remembered them well. But the result was that passages they cited frequently contained mistaken characters. Take, for instance, Mencius's citations from the *Odes* and *History*: they were often mistaken, because he had nothing to base himself on but was simply recalling from memory. (10.170)

57. Students today, when they have read a text it as if they had never read it, and when they haven't read it it's as if they had. (10.171)

58. In reading, you must not be of a mind-heart anxious to finish, for as soon as you are, the mind-heart will simply fix on the blank page at the end of the text, which will be of no benefit at all! (10.173)

59. In reading, you must set up curricular limits. Manage it [the reading] as if it were farm work. In farming there are boundary lines. Learning is the same. Beginning students today do not appreciate this principle. At the outset, they're extremely energetic, but they gradually grow indolent, until, in the end, they understand nothing at all. This is just because they do not establish curricular limits at the outset. (10.174)

60. Nowadays people who genuinely read are few, owing to the pernicious influence of the examination essay. In picking up a text to read, they have already made up their minds to seek what is unusual in it and pay little attention to its original meaning. Once they have found the unusual in it, they mimic it in their writing of the examination essays. The result is that they perform well, but this is their only use for the text. (10.175)

61. People beyond midlife need not read much, but they should ponder somewhat over what little they do read, and moral principle will naturally become clear. (10.175)

62. In reading, do not look for meaning on the page alone. You need to turn within and look for meaning in yourself. Since the Qin-Han period no one has spoken of this, and people have merely sought understanding from the text and not in themselves. What we have yet to understand for ourselves, the sages have explained in texts. It is best that we use their words to seek it in ourselves. (11.181)

63. The problem students have in reading is that they're intent on moving forward and unwilling to go back and reread. The more they move ahead, the greater their misunderstanding. It would be better if they were to go back and review what they have read. The problem generally is that they stick to their original reading and are unwilling to let go of it. It's like hearing litigation: if beforehand the mind-heart supports proposition B, it will just search for the wrongs in A; and if beforehand it supports proposition A, it will simply find the wrongs in B. Better to set

aside one's views of A and B and carefully examine both. Then one may be capable of distinguishing right from wrong. Hengqu [Zhang Zai] said, "Wash away the old understandings and bring forth new ideas."[16] This statement is right on target. If you don't wash away old understandings, where can new ideas arise? Nowadays students are prone to two types of defects: one is to be ruled by personal opinions; the other is to embrace received theories. Though you may want to shake free of these, they'll naturally chase after you. (11.185)

64. In learning, don't skip steps and don't be careless. For you will be wasting your energy. Follow the right sequence and your understanding will be as it should. If you come to understand one Classic intimately, other texts will be easy to read. (11.187)

65. When we read the Six Classics, it's just as if there were no Six Classics; if we simply look for the moral principle in ourselves, principle will be easy to understand. (11.188)

66. In learning you must first establish the great foundation. At the outset focus on the essential, in the middle on broad learning, and in the end again on the most essential: Mencius said, "Learn widely and go into what you have learned in detail so that in the end you can return to the essential."[17] It's for this reason that we must first read the *Analects*, the *Book of Mencius*, the *Great Learning*, and the *Mean* in order to examine the intentions of the sages and worthies; we then read the histories in order to examine evidence of preservation and ruin, and order and disorder. And we then read the thinkers of the hundred schools to appreciate their various faults. There's a natural sequence to these steps—and we mustn't skip over any of them. Today, students often find pleasure in what's essential but don't pursue breadth. I don't know how, without pursuing breadth, they can investigate the essential. The person who favors the essential and these days becomes a Buddhist priest will apprehend his one body alone. And then there's the person who focuses only on the

pursuit of breadth and never returns to what is essential: he investigates one institution today and another one tomorrow, laboring vainly on what is "practical." His fault is more serious than the essentialist who neglects breadth. In essence, however, neither type benefits. (11.188)

67. In whatever we read, there needs be an order. Take, for instance, a paragraph of three sentences: focus on the first sentence until you understand it completely; next focus on the second and then on the third, until you understand them. Afterward go over the whole paragraph, investigate its meaning, and ruminate on it. If you still don't completely understand it, look at explanations of it by earlier generations, and then read through it a second time. You must understand where it will improve *you* and only then will it be of any benefit. (11.189)

68. They were talking about the method of reading and Zhu said: First read the text ten or more times and you'll get 40 to 50 percent of its meaning. Afterward, read the annotations on it and you'll get another 20 to 30 percent. Turn again to the classical text and you'll get another 10 to 20 percent. Earlier I didn't understand the *Mencius* because its paragraphs were so long. Then I read it as just described, and though at first the paragraphs were long, I found that the meaning cohered from beginning to end. (11.190)

69. In reading, generally you should examine most closely those places where there are differing explanations. Let's say A explains a passage one way. Take explanation A in hand and probe it through and through. B explains it this way. Take explanation B in hand and probe it through and through. When you have finished with both explanations and critically examined them, the truth is bound to emerge. (11.192)

70. In explicating a book, you must first restore the original text, and next recover its original meaning. Adding unimportant words does no real harm, but you cannot add important ones.

It is precisely these substantive words that people today add. (11.194)

MINDFUL READING

71. In reading you must keep your mind-heart glued to the text. Only when each and every sentence and each and every character fall into place can you begin to deliberate beneficially. In general, students must collect their mind-hearts so that they are still and pure and, in everyday life—in times both of tranquility and activity—they don't become reckless or confused. Only then will they understand the text in all of its fine detail. Reading like this they will get the essentials. (11.177)

72. In reading today people are often muddled and lax when they approach a text and thus take little care with it. Best, therefore, if students collected their thoughts in some tranquil spot and afterward proceeded to read the text with an open mind-heart (*xuxin*). Its meaning then would become entirely clear. (11.177)

73. In the past Mr. Chen Li was distressed that he had no power of memory. One day, when reading the passage from the *Mencius*, "The great end of learning is nothing else but to seek for the lost mind-heart,"[18] he was suddenly enlightened and said, "If my mind-heart is not retrieved how will I remember text?" He thereupon shut the door and practiced quiet-sitting and for more than one hundred days did no reading. Having retrieved his lost mind-heart, he turned to reading and, with but a glance, absorbed everything! (11.177)

74. In reading it's frequently because their mind-hearts are not present that students do not understand the principle of the Way. The words of the sages and worthies are originally intelligible of themselves; give them but a little attention and you'll come to understand them on your own. If you concentrate your mind-heart, you couldn't possibly not understand. (11.177)

75. When the mind-heart is not settled, it won't understand principle. Today, when we are about to read, it's critical that we settle the mind-heart first, so that it becomes like still water or a clear mirror. A cloudy mirror can't reflect anything. (11.177)

76. If your will (*zhi*) is not firmly fixed, how can you read? (11.177)

77. There is a method to reading: Simply scrub clean the mind-heart and afterward go read. If you do not understand the text, put it down for a moment, wait until your thoughts have cleared, then pick it up and read it again. Nowadays, though, we talk about the need to open the mind-heart. But how is the mind-heart to be opened? Now we just have to take the mind-heart and focus it on the text. (11.177)

78. Reading must be an experience meaningful to the self. It must not be just a matter of looking over the characters or of "helping [the mind-heart] to grow."[19] (11.181)

79. When taking a break from reading, practice quiet-sitting so that your mind-heart becomes calm and your psychophysical stuff becomes settled. You'll understand the principle of the Way with increasing clarity. (11.187)

80. If someone who has nothing to do each day and has his food prepared for him spent half of the day in quiet-sitting and the other half reading; and if he did this for one or two years, he would need not worry about making progress. (116.2806)

81. Generally, in reading a text, we need to recite it aloud and not simply think it over. When our mouths recite it, our mind-hearts relax and the meaning emerges naturally. When I first started learning, I did exactly this. There's no other way. (11.179)

82. In reading you must open your mind-heart and make the text relevant to you. Only when you open your mind-heart are you able to grasp the meaning of the sages and worthies; and when you make the text relevant to you, the words of the sages and worthies will not be empty. (11.178)

83. In reading a text you must open your mind-heart. Don't approach the text with preconceived ideas or, in no time, you'll make a lot of mistakes. He further said: Open your mind-heart and make the text relevant to you. By opening your mind-heart you'll understand principle clearly; by making the text relevant to you, you'll naturally grasp its meaning for yourself. (11.179)

84. The words of the sages are all heavenly principle just as they are, and basically easy to understand. It's simply that people don't approach them with an open mind-heart and so grasp them but superficially. With no real understanding of them, they explain them using their own personal views, taking them for the views of the sages. (11.179)

85. Someone asked: What do you do when in reading you become confused by a multitude of views?

Zhu replied: You need to keep an open mind-heart and read each view in turn, first reading this view and then reading that view. Keep reading and right and wrong, good and bad, will naturally become clear. It is like a person who wants to know whether another person is good or bad. He will keep an eye on him whatever he does, observing his words and actions and then as a matter of course will know whether he is good or bad. He also said, Wash away the old opinions and bring forth a new understanding. (11.180)

86. Depend on the text when inspecting a text, depend on the object when inspecting an object. Do not approach them with preconceived ideas. (11.181)

87. In learning, we must read for ourselves, so that our understanding is personally meaningful. Nowadays, people read simply for the sake of the civil service examinations. Once they pass the examinations, they read for the sake of learning to write miscellaneous prose. And the eminent among them read for the sake of learning to write ancient-style prose. In all these instances, they're reading for external reasons. (11.182)

88. Whenever you read a text, you must first come to an understanding of its words and afterward look to see if its views accord with principle or not. If they do, they're right; if not, they're wrong. People today often first have an idea in their own mind-hearts and then take what others have said to explain that idea. What doesn't conform with their idea they forcibly make to conform. (11.185)

89. Students must not compromise the words of the sages and worthies with their own ideas. (11.185)

90. In reading, when you have no doubts, encourage them; and when you do have doubts, do your best to have none. Only when you reach this point will there be progress. (11.186)

91. The problem with people is that they know to doubt the views of others but not their own. If they were to try to reproach themselves as they reproach others, they might understand some of their own faults. (11.187)

92. If in doing their lessons people don't focus and instead read here and there, their mind-hearts will stray and they won't understand the principle of the Way. They must read the *Analects*, concentrating only on the *Analects*, and then read the *Mencius*, concentrating only on the *Mencius*. When reading this paragraph, they must not be looking at the next paragraph; and when reading this sentence, they cannot be reading the next sentence; and when considering this character they must not be looking at the next character. If they do this, they'll be focused and their efforts will be successful. If their reading isn't focused and orderly, though they might give months and years to it, there is no hope of their gaining a thorough understanding. Formerly, I seized on this method, and continue with it to this day. In thinking this over, I find this really is the only method—there is no other. (11.189)

93. Once principle is clear to you, you'll even get something out of reading Shen [Buhai] and Han [Feizi].[20] (11.190)

94. In reading, people generally should keep their mind-hearts open [*xuxin*] and read with a singleness of purpose until they're intimately familiar with the text. They must not come to it with a preconceived understanding. They should read the text through, ponder it deeply, and become intimately familiar until its words become like their own. This is the right way to read. But in reading today one type of student is intent only on cultivating his prose composition and another type wants what he says to be so novel and unusual that what others say can't compare to what he has said. These are serious defects in the students. (11.191)

When Zhu Xi proclaims to his students—taking some of them by surprise no doubt—that "reading is a secondary matter for students" (10.161), he is reminding them that reading is simply a means by which people can hope to become more moral, to realize the moral potential endowed in them at birth.

Much of chapters 12 and 13 of the *Classified Conversations* is given over to the role mind plays in realizing this innate goodness. Drawing again on Zhang Zai's proposition that "the mind governs the nature and emotions," Zhu Xi describes the mind in these chapters as the arbiter of human beings' moral predicament. In his words, it is "our master," dictating whether we give ourselves to the cultivation of our inherently moral nature or succumb to the allure of selfish desires. The mind, Zhu suggests, is the indeterminate element in human beings, "waxing and waning between heavenly principle and human desire." (13.225) To be sure, our original mind is good, inherently capable of discerning right from wrong, as Mencius asserted (2A.6). But, as it encounters the myriad things and affairs in the world, it can give rise to desire. And when desire becomes excessive and imbalanced, it "covers over" or obstructs the good human nature. This is why Zhu is insistent in conversations with students that they must "preserve the mind," "hold on to it," "control it," "awaken it," "keep it alert," and so on. Human beings, it appears, are at constant risk of losing moral direction, of being led astray by emotions and desires that arise as we naturally go about our lives.

The mind then must be vigilant. To this end, Zhu Xi, inspired by Cheng Yi before him, admonishes students to be *jing*, translated in this volume as "reverentially attentive." It is hard to find an entirely satisfactory English equivalent for the term. To be *jing* is to be fully and deeply attentive to whatever it is that one is doing. It is to concentrate one's entire mental energy on the thing or affair at hand. And that concentration is mirrored in one's physical demeanor. Being reverentially attentive is to see and experience things and affairs in the world without the slightest distraction—to see things as they truly are. "If you practice reverential attentiveness," Zhu remarks, "heavenly principle will always be bright and as a matter of course human desire will be restrained and dissipate" (12.210).

Zhu Xi here is urging his Confucian followers to engage the world more seriously and mindfully. He wants them to go beyond their superficial experience of the world and "investigate things" (*gewu*), a term he adopts from the brief Classic, the *Greater Learning*. Zhu makes much of this term in his philosophical system, glossing it to mean "probing the principle in affairs and things." By probing principle, students will come to see things and affairs in the world around them as they truly are—and respond to things and affairs just as they should.

It is essential to appreciate that the investigation of things is not principally a "scientific" exercise—that is, its goal is not to accumulate facts about things in the world. It is a moral one. Because principle in the universe is one, to apprehend principle through the investigation of affairs and things in the world out there is to apprehend the principle that is within us. It is to escape from our moral predicament and realize our full moral potential.

A. Holding on to the Mind-Heart

1. Since antiquity sages and worthies have all considered the mind-heart to be the root. (12.199)

2. The myriad words of the sages and worthies ask only that people not lose their original mind-hearts. (12.199)

3. If the mind-heart be not preserved, your person will be without a master. (12.199)

4. As soon as you leave your gates, there are tens of thousands of paths and roads. If you are without a master, how will you find your way? (12.199).

5. A student's effort rests simply in awakening it [the mind-heart].

Someone asked: When a person lets it run wild, and then himself seeks to gather it in, isn't this "to awaken" it?

Zhu replied: We let it run wild only because we're muddled. If we're able to awaken it, then of course we're not muddled; and if we're not muddled, then naturally we will not let it run wild. (12.200)

6. The mind-heart is just this one mind-heart. It isn't that we use one mind-heart to control another mind-heart. What we call preserving it and gathering it in is simply to awaken it. (12.200)

7. Each person has only the one mind that serves as master. It must be kept awake at all times. (12.201)

8. Generally speaking, gather the mind-heart in and you will be 80 to 90 percent there. Still, in looking for the principle of the Way you will meet with obstacles. Give your full attention to them. In your learning you have to focus the mind-heart. When you're attending to one particular matter, attend to this one particular matter alone. When walking, simply be mindful of walking; when sitting simply be mindful of sitting. (12.201)

9. In learning, before inquiring about true knowledge and vigorous action, a student must collect his mind-heart and give

it a place to settle. If in gathering it in he places it in the midst
of moral principle, it'll be largely free of reckless thoughts, and
after a while will be light with material desire and heavy with
moral principle. It's essential that moral principle in the mind-
heart outweigh material desire. The mind-heart is like a scale
with a low and high end. Once it starts to appreciate moral principle it can't stop itself even if it wanted to; it will not have a chance
to swing back in the direction of material desire. If in "holding
it fast and letting it go, preserving it and losing it"[1] he has no master [that is, a collected mind-heart], we might explain [true
knowledge and vigorous action] to him but it would be of no benefit. (12.201)

10. If today in our leisure time we make a point of gathering
in the mind-heart, we'll achieve the state "before pleasure, anger,
sorrow, and joy have arisen"[2]—and be in full accord with heavenly principle. When affairs and things arise, we'll have a clear
sense of right and wrong: right is heavenly principle, wrong vio-
lates heavenly principle. Keeping the mind-heart gathered in at
all times is like having in hand a scale to weigh things. (12.202)

11. Students must seek their lost mind-hearts. Afterward
they'll recognize the goodness of their human nature. Human
nature is always good; it's simply because a person has let go of
his mind-heart that he falls into evil. "What heaven has conferred
is called human nature" means that heaven's decree resides in a
person and that he's entirely good. "After they have arisen and
attained due measure,"[3] this too is goodness; when they do not
attain due measure—this is evil. Human nature is perfectly complete. And, can what's allotted by the yin and yang psychophysical stuff and the five phases possibly not be good? It's when people themselves do not move in the direction of goodness that
they do evil. Han Yu argued that after Mencius it [the tradition]
was no longer handed down,[4] and this was because students of
later generations gave no attention to the mind-heart. What Yao

and Shun transmitted was nothing more than a discussion of the "human mind-heart" and the "mind-heart of the Way" and "being discriminating, undivided, and holding on to the mean."[5] Under heaven there are simply the two extremes of good and evil. For instance, when yin and yang reside in heaven, the wind is gentle and the sun comfortably warm, and the ten thousand things send forth their shoots, this is the meaning of good; and when yin is in power the ten thousand things wither. Evil in man has a similar effect. The principle of heaven and earth will definitely restrain the yin psychophysical stuff and typically doesn't allow it to triumph. When good and evil are mixed together, students need to disentangle them and not allow the shoots of goodness growing in a patch of evil to be cut down. If in their day-to-day movement and rest they constantly examine themselves, preserving and nourishing it [the mind-heart], it naturally will fully develop. (12.203)

12. The mind-heart—unprejudiced, spiritual, and conscious—is one. But that there is a distinction between the "human mind-heart" and the "mind-heart of the Way" is due to this: the mind-heart at times arises in the self-centeredness of the psychophysical being (*xingqi* 形氣) and at times originates in the perfect impartiality of the moral nature decreed by heaven, so the resulting consciousnesses are different. Hence the mind-heart can be precarious and unsettled, or abstruse and almost imperceptible. Yet all men have a psychophysical being, so even the very wisest will always have a human mind-heart; and all men have a moral nature, so even the very stupidest will always have a mind-heart of the Way. If the human mind-heart and the mind-heart of the Way become mixed in the heart and one does not know how to control them, the precarious will become even more precarious, the imperceptible will become even more imperceptible, and the impartiality of the heavenly principle in the end will be unable to overcome the selfishness of human desires. "Be

discriminating" means to distinguish between the human mind-heart and mind-heart of the Way so that they do not become mixed. "Be undivided" means to protect the perfect impartiality of the original mind-heart so that it does not take leave of one. Should one devote oneself without interruption to these matters, making certain that the mind-heart of the Way always acts as master of the body and the human mind-heart always obeys its orders, the precarious will become settled and the almost imperceptible will become manifest. And in activity and tranquility, in words and actions, one will not err in going either too far or not far enough.[6]

13. In a bright person, it is bright. Others must nurture it. "Nurturing" it isn't to work away at it with a hammer and chisel but is simply to keep the mind-heart open and tranquil, and after a time it will naturally become bright. (12.204)

14. Someone said that it's at rest that we normally preserve and nurture it [the mind-heart].

Zhu said: This is mistaken. Whether in motion or at rest there's no time we don't nurture it. (12.204)

15. As for the mind-heart, it's best that, whenever it must respond to an affair, it be just as it is when there is no affair. (12.204)

16. The human mind-heart is originally bright. It's just that it gets covered over by things and affairs and can't get out from under them. As a consequence, illumining principle is difficult. Let people strip away the things that are covering it and wait for it to come out on its own and take a look around a couple of times. Having summoned the mind-heart they'll naturally recognize right from wrong and good from evil. (12.205)

17. A person must examine his mistaken mind-heart with the unmistaken mind-heart. The unmistaken mind-heart is the original mind-heart; the mistaken one is this original mind-heart lost. (12.205)

18. Only when the mind-heart achieves just the right balance is it capable of knowing the goodness of human nature. (12.205)

19. The effort required by students entails pruning away superficial and extraneous thoughts. (12.206)

20. Generally, in learning you must first brighten the mind-heart and only afterward will you be capable of learning. It's comparable to lighting a fire: you must first fan the flame and afterward add the firewood and then the flame will grow bright. If you first add the firewood and afterward fan the flame, the flame will go out. It's like our contemporaries who without looking into the Six Classics probe into the examination-style essay. (12.206)

21. Confucius said "subdue the self and return to ritual";[7] the *Mean* said "let the mean and harmony be fully realized," "honor the inborn virtuous nature," and "follow the path of inquiry and learning";[8] the *Greater Learning* said "keep the inborn luminous virtue unobscured";[9] and the *Classic of History* said "the human mind-heart is precarious, the mind-heart of the Way is almost imperceptible. Be discriminating, be undivided, that you may sincerely hold fast the mean."[10] The myriad words of the sages and worthies simply instruct people to understand heavenly principle and extinguish human desire. Once heavenly principle is bright, there's no more need for explanations. Human nature is originally bright, but like a pearl immersed in dirty water, its brightness may not be evident; dispose of the dirty water and the pearl will naturally become bright as before. When we ourselves understand that human desire is covering it [our heavenly principle], its brightness will shine. Apply yourself here with diligence and resolve, making the investigation of things part of your effort. Today investigate one thing and tomorrow investigate another. It will be just like a guerilla army surrounding [its enemy] and laying siege; human desires will disperse on their

own. This is why in explaining the term "reverential attentive-ness," Master Cheng simply says that there is a bright thing right here. Take these words "reverential attentiveness" to resist the enemy; forever maintain reverential attentiveness right here and human desires naturally will be unable to show themselves. Con-fucius said, "The practice of true goodness rests with oneself, not with others."[11] The crucial point is right here! (12.207)

22. The practice of true goodness is the means of preserving whole the virtue of the mind-heart. Now, the virtue of the mind-heart in its wholeness is nothing but heavenly principle, which cannot but be harmed by human desire. Consequently, in prac-ticing true goodness, one must have the wherewithal to subdue selfish desires and thereby return to ritual. Then, all affairs will be a matter of heavenly principle, and the virtue of the original mind-heart will return to its wholeness in one's person.[12]

23. Previous generations all talked casually about the char-acter *jing* (reverential attentiveness). Master Cheng alone invested it with great meaning. People simply need to seek their lost mind-hearts. But what is it that constitutes the mind-heart? It's noth-ing but reverential attentiveness. As soon as someone is reveren-tially attentive, this mind-heart is present in his person. (12.209)

24. Learning is really complicated for people and requires skill. Thus, Master Cheng spoke of "holding on to reverential attentiveness," which is to arouse the mind-heart so that it becomes bright and understands all affairs. Over time, it natu-rally will grow vigorous and strong. (12.209)

25. The practice of reverential attentiveness is of greatest sig-nificance in the Confucian school. From beginning to end there mustn't be even a moment's interruption. (12.210)

26. Practice reverential attentiveness and the myriad mani-festations of principle will be complete in you. (12.210)

27. Reverential attentiveness overcomes the hundred moral depravities. (12.210)

28. Just practice reverential attentiveness and the mind-heart will be one. (12.210)

29. Reverential attentiveness is simply the mind-heart itself acting as master. (12.210)

30. If you practice reverential attentiveness, heavenly principle will always be bright, and as a matter of course human desire will be restrained and dissipate. (12.210)

31. Reverential attentiveness is not just for sitting. When you lift your feet to walk you need this mind-heart to be present. (12.211)

32. Reverential attentiveness is not to sit like a lump, with your ears hearing nothing, your eyes seeing nothing, and your mind-heart thinking nothing. It's not this that we call reverential attentiveness. It's simply to be watchful and daring not to lose restraint. If this is the case, the mind-heart will be collected, as if it is fearful of something. And if it's like this at all times, it will naturally be discriminating. Preserve this mind-heart and you can engage in learning. (12.211)

33. Someone asked: How does one work at being reverentially attentive?

Zhu replied: It is simply to have no wild ideas within, and no wild behavior without. (12.211)

34. "Sit as though you were impersonating an ancestor, stand as though you were performing a sacrifice." "The head is to be upright, the eyes looking straight ahead, the feet steady, the hands respectful, the mouth still, the bearing solemn"[13]—all of these are aspects of reverential attentiveness. (12.212)

35. Generally, if you don't take firm hold of it, you will not be truly good. The human mind-heart being clear, open, and settled is the essence of being truly good. If you don't take firm hold of it, selfish desires will seize it and shake it into confusion. This being the case, take firm hold of it and just be diligent in practicing reverential attentiveness. (12.213)

36. Someone asked: How does a person be true and reverentially attentive and rid himself of desires?

Zhu replied: This is the ultimate! Being true is to cast aside falsehoods; being reverentially attentive is to cast aside laxness. As for desires, they simply need to be restrained. (12.213)

37. Practicing reverential attentiveness is similar to the work of tending a field and keeping it well watered; "subduing the self"[14] is to remove the weeds from the field. (12.214)

38. Reverential attentiveness means to hold to this with no wavering; righteousness means to do to that in perfect accord with what is right. (12.216)

39. Yizhi asked: Preserving and nurturing [the mind-heart] depend largely on quiescence, right?

Zhu said: It need not be the case. Confucius had people make an effort to preserve and nurture everywhere it would be useful. Although today it is said that quiescence is the master, it isn't that we are to abandon affairs and things in the pursuit of quiescence. Being human, we naturally serve our ruler and kin, engage with our friends, care for our wives and children, and manage our household servants. We cannot renounce these responsibilities, shut our gates, and practice quiet-sitting, and, then, when affairs and things arise, just say, "Wait until I'm done preserving and nurturing!" Neither, though, can we just attend endlessly to affairs and things. It's best if we consider putting a stop to both of these [extremes]. (12.218)

40. In times of quiescence think not about activity; in times of activity think not about quiescence. (12.219)

41. The human body is simply active or quiescent. Quiescence is the root of nurturing activity, and activity is the means by which quiescence is practiced. In activity there is quiescence, as in the passage "when the feelings have arisen and attained due proportion"[15]—this is quiescence within activity. (12.219)

42. Someone asked: Take the two words, "activity" and "quiescence." In the course of a person's day, moments of "quiescence" are few and moments of "activity" are many.

Zhu responded: In moments of activity a sage is always quiescent; by contrast, in moments of activity the multitude are confused and in turmoil. When people today want to do something, they are unable to concentrate on the one thing alone or handle it with ease. When the thought occurs to them that they'd like to do this, they would also like to do that—which is why in times of activity there is no quiescence. (12.219)

42. Principle in things and in our mind-heart is fundamentally one. In neither is it deficient in the slightest. It's essential only that we respond to things, that is all. Things and the mind-heart share this same principle. (12.220)

43. After doing quiet-sitting for a while, we're muddled and exhausted, and unable to think. And when get up to go we feel agitated and tense. (12.221)

B. Subduing Desires and Actualizing Moral Principle

44. Studying it extensively isn't as good as knowing its essentials; and knowing its essentials isn't as good as actually practicing them. (13.222)

45. When people are incapable of putting into practice the principle of the Way, it's simply because the principle of the Way in us has not been fully realized. We should not complain that it's because we are incapable of putting it into practice; instead we should turn within and seek to bring the Way to full realization there. (13.223)

46. Here, I will lecture less and have you practice more. It will fall to you to heed, examine, and nurture all matters on your own. It will fall to you to read on your own, and it will fall

to you to investigate the principle of the Way on your own. I
will just serve as a guide, a person who certifies what you do and,
when you have doubts or difficulties, talks them over with you.
(13.223)

47. There is heavenly principle and there is human desire. It
seems because this heavenly principle must have a place to settle
that when it doesn't settle as it should, human desire arises.
(13.223)

48. As for the human mind-heart, if heavenly principle is preserved, human desire will disappear. But should human desire
prevail, heavenly principle will be extinguished. Never do heavenly principle and human desire mix. It is essential that students
fully recognize this and be watchful over themselves. (13.224)

49. It's simply because there's strife between heavenly principle and human desire that Master Zhou [Dunyi] speaks point-
edly of *ji* 幾, "incipient movements not yet visible on the outside."
This being the case, in distinguishing between the two we have
to be quick, which is why Hengqu [Zhang Zai] always spoke of
"anticipating." (13.224).

50. When not darkened by creaturely desires we will be in full
accord with heavenly principle. (13.224)

51. Humans have but this one mind-heart. If it's right today
and wrong tomorrow it is isn't that the right one has been
replaced with the wrong one. If it's bad today and good tomorrow, it isn't that the good one has been replaced with the bad
one. There's just one mind-heart, but we have to keep in mind
that it waxes and wanes between heavenly principle and human
desire. For thousands of years past and the thousands of years to
come it is this one mind-heart alone that constantly operates in
tandem with heaven and earth. When you read, you need not
bother to cite supporting material for your understanding.
This is to become entangled for the sake of others. If you're
really doing it for your own sake, then you have to test what you

read against your own mind-heart, understanding that what the sages and worthies say today is no different from your mind-heart today. This is the right practice! (13.225)

52. Today just distinguish between human desire and heavenly principle. When this one is in large supply, that one is sure to be in short supply; and when this one is in short supply, that one is sure to be in large supply. (13.225)

53. Before we know to learn, our mind-heart is full of human desire. Once we know to learn, heavenly principle naturally emerges and human desire gradually subsides—which is a good thing, for sure. Subdue one pile of desires after another. We definitely can't have big desires; as for minute ones, we need to be especially watchful. (13.225)

54. Moral principle is something our mind-hearts naturally possess. When we lose it, though, we don't know how to recover it. Wealth and position are things external to our bodies; we seek them, fearful we will not obtain them. Suppose we were to obtain them; they'd be of no benefit at all to the mind-heart. And we can't even be sure of obtaining them! As for moral principle, if we do seek it, we will get it.[16] And once we're capable of not losing what we have we can become sages or worthies. The beneficial and the harmful are extremely clear. The impartiality of the human mind-heart is invariably obscured by human desire—so do not let go of it. Let's just keep watch over these two alternatives all the time. When we understand clearly, we will be sure to give due consideration to the one and urgently rid ourselves of the other. (13.225)

55. Goodness and righteousness are inherent in the human mind-heart; the mind-heart bent on profit is born of comparison between ourselves and others. (13.228)

56. To manage affairs in accord with the true and great principle of the Way under heaven is to be impartial; to manage them in accord with self-centeredness is to be partial. (13.228)

57. Just focus on right and wrong, and that's enough. He added: What's right is principle. (13.228)

58. The effort required of the student is to pursue right. The principle of all under heaven is nothing but the two alternatives, right and wrong. Following what is right is to do good, according with what is wrong is to do evil. In serving parents you must be filial; if you are not, it's not the Way of serving parents. In serving the ruler you must be loyal; if you are not, it's not the Way of serving a ruler. In all matters you must look into right and wrong, choose the right, and then practice it. In teaching others, the Sage was unceasing in illuminating this principle. [When the Master said in *Analects* 2.4], "At fifteen I set my mind-heart on learning," what he set his mind-heart on was just this; [when he said], "at thirty I stood on my own," what he stood on was just this, and [when he said] "at forty I had no doubts," he meant that for him there was no other principle of the Way— and that he had simply come to understand this clearly and to practice it. To be a sage or a worthy rests entirely in this. The Sage feared, though, that other people would not understand and so explained it in all variety of ways and wherever he could. Could students possibly not know the right choice to make! Today, if in reading you're unable to understand this principle fully, it's simply that your mind-heart is crude and your thoughts diffuse. When analyzing the meaning of a text, turn it over and over with an open mind-heart. The sages' words are tightly interwoven, like plaits of silken hair. If you simply pass over them with your eyes, how can you possibly understand them in all their profundity? And consequently you'll miss the meaning of the sages. (13.229)

59. I've said that today's ways of teaching and guiding others are all mistaken. There is not a person who is clear about how to do it. Those who explain the principle of the Way, explain it all wrong—their explanations are misguided. And those who

compose literary essays just learn to compose bad essays, while those who compose poetry don't recognize good poetry. As for the explanations of Chan Buddhism, they are not the Chan of the original Buddha; and the cultivation and nurturing is not the cultivation and nurturing of the way of Lao and Zhuang. Nothing is right! (13.235)

60. Only when a certain principle exists does a certain thing or affair exist. Take grass and trees: only when their seed exists will they produce grass and trees. Take people: only when have a mind-heart to carry out a certain matter will they accomplish this matter. If they are not of this mind-heart, how would they be able to accomplish this matter? (13.236)

61. The mind-heart inclined to do the good is the true one; the mind-heart inclined to do the bad is the false one. If it becomes contaminated within by that false one, the true one will likewise be ruined. (13.236)

62. That people become miserable over poverty and humble status and anxious about wealth and high position is simply because they don't understand this principle of the Way. If they did, poverty and humble status would be incapable of diminishing them and wealth and high position would add nothing to them. They need only appreciate this principle of the Way. (13.241)

RECONCILING LEARNING TO BE MORAL AND LEARNING FOR THE EXAMINATIONS

63. Moral principle is what all human mind-hearts share. Investigating it is easy for people to do. Examination preparation is an external affair and, by contrast, is difficult to do. It's a pity that exam preparation has ruined so many people! (13.243)

64. Literati must first distinguish between the examinations and canonical reading—which is less important and which more.

If 70 percent of one's determination is given to reading and 30 percent to the examinations, that'll be just fine. But if 70 percent is given to the examinations and 30 percent to reading, the 30 percent is certain to be overcome by the 70 percent. How much more if one's determination is given entirely to the exams! As the person grows older, it will be of no use to him at all—doing nothing for his self-improvement. The Sage's teaching are simply for the sake of oneself. (13.243)

65. Those who specialize in writing examination-style essays mimic the words of the sages and worthies in their words. So when, for example, they speak of incorruptibility, they're able to speak of it eloquently; and when they speak of righteousness, they're again able speak of it eloquently. And yet in their own conduct, they're of course not incorruptible nor are they righteous. This is because they merely take the many words of the sages and worthies and put them to paper. Their incorruptibility is the incorruptibility spoken of in response to a posed question; their righteousness is the righteousness spoken of in response to a posed question. Both are trivial matters of no real personal relevance to them. (13.244)

66. Zhu said to someone: You say not to read classical texts and focus only on reading examination-style essays. In the end, what sort of person do you hope to become? If you take the examinations and repeatedly fail, with age you'll grow melancholic and wander about the village aimlessly. And as a result of skill in the examination-style essay, should you become an official, you'd just be crude; you wouldn't even bother to say you want to serve the country and the people, to promote what is beneficial and abolish what is harmful, or to fulfill responsibly the duties of your office. You'd be obsessed, wanting only to advance, and stabbing others in the back for gain. In seeking promotion and recommendation there's nothing you would not do. (13.245)

67. They were discussing the relative importance of cultivating the self and sitting for the examinations, and Zhu said: There are some today who are abandoned in their disloyalty and unfiliality; they feign incorruptibility and a sense of shame, and they flout established norms. It's not only they who think nothing of it. Authorities think nothing of it, and poor villagers think nothing of it. I have no idea how customs have fallen into such disrepair. It's awful—I'm completely horrified by it. (13.245)

68. Not sitting for the examinations is a small matter. And yet, these days, when people say they aren't going to sit for them they hold it up as some great achievement. As I see it, if they put their mind-hearts to understanding the principle of the Way, soon the examinations would not be a bother to them at all. And without even realizing it, they would come to regard wealth, honor, prosperity, and notoriety as inconsequential. (13.245)

69. Someone asked whether exam preparation interferes with efforts at true learning.

Zhu replied: Master Cheng said, "Do not fear that it will interfere with efforts at true learning; fear only that it will rob you of your determination to learn."[17] Spend ten days of each month on examination preparation, and the other twenty days on cultivating learning. But if your determination to learn is shaken, there will indeed be no remedy. (13.246)

70. Preparation for the examinations doesn't harm learning. When did previous generations ever refrain from taking the exams? It's simply because people today have unsettled mind-hearts that harm is done. As soon as the mind-heart is given to thoughts of success and failure, understanding of the text and its import will all be mistaken. (13.246)

71. He was discussing the examinations and said: It isn't that the examinations are a trouble to people, it's that people become troubled by the examinations. A scholar of superior understanding reads the texts of the sages and worthies and on the basis of

his understanding writes his examination essay answers, putting aside considerations of success and failure and gain and loss. Even if he were to compete in the examinations every day, he would not be troubled by them. If Confucius were to be reborn today, he would not avoid competing in the examinations. Nor would they trouble him in the least. (13.246)

72. Yizhi said: Xu Shuzhong[18] is too eager in preparing for the examinations.

Zhu replied: His family is impoverished and his parents old; he can't avoid competing in the exams, so it is best to let him prepare for them. Preparing for the exams does no harm. It is only if one is obsessed with thoughts of success and failure that harm to the Way is done. (13.247)

73. Nowadays people are incapable of cultivating themselves. As soon as they become literati, they strive without stop to win office. In office, they're further distressed that they aren't advancing and run around anxiously, not resting for even a day. How can they compare to the humble scholar living in a mountain retreat? The Way and righteousness fill his person. And because the Way and righteousness fill his person, what could possibly entangle him! (13.247)

A sage doesn't know that he himself is a sage. (13.232)

Glossary of Key Terms

cheng 誠 (authentic, sincere)
dao 道 (the Way, path)
daoli 道理 (principle of the Way)
daoxin 道心 (mind-heart of the Way *or* Dao mind-heart)
Daoxue 道學 (Learning *or* School of the Way)
dushufa 讀書法 (method of reading)
gewu 格物 (investigation of things)
gui 鬼 (*gui* spirit, ghost)
guishen 鬼神 (spirits, spirit beings)
hun 魂 (heavenly soul)
jing 敬 (reverential attentiveness)
jing 靜 (quiescence, tranquility, stillness)
jingshen 精神 (vital spirit)
junzi 君子 (morally superior person)
li 理 (principle)
li 禮 (propriety, ritual, rites)
ling 靈 (spiritually efficacious, numen, intelligence)
ming 命 (decree)
po 魄 (earthly soul)
qi 氣 (psychophysical stuff)
qizhi zhi xing 氣質之性 (psychophysical nature)

qing 情 (emotions, feelings)

qiongli 窮理 (probing principle)

ren 仁 (true goodness)

renxin 人心 (human mind-heart)

shen 神 (*shen* spirit, the expansive spirit)

taiji 太極 (supreme ultimate, great ultimate)

ti 體 (substance)

tian 天 (heaven, nature)

tianli 天理 (heavenly principle)

weiji zhi xue 為己之學 (learning for one's own sake)

weiren zhi xue 為人之學 (learning for the sake of others)

wusi 無私 (without self-interest)

wuwei 無為 (act without deliberation)

xin 心 (mind-heart)

xing 性 (nature)

xiushen 修身 (self-cultivation)

xuxin 虛心 (an open or unprejudiced mind-heart; to open the mind-heart)

yi 意 (intention)

yi 義 (righteous, righteousness)

yili 義理 (moral principle)

yin 陰

yang 陽

yong 用 (function, operation)

zhi 質 (matter)

zhi 智 (wisdom)

zhi 志 (will, determination, ambition)

zhizhi 致知 (extension of knowledge)

Notes

INTRODUCTION

1. On Zhu Xi's government service, see Conrad M. Schirokauer, "Chu Hsi's Political Career: A Study in Ambivalence," in *Confucian Personalities*, ed. Arthur Wright and Denis Twitchett (Stanford, CA: Stanford University Press, 1962).

2. For example, Zhu Xi, *Zhu Xi ji* [Collected works of Zhu Xi], ed. Guo Qi and Yin Bo (Chengdu: Sichuan jiaoyu chubanshe, 1996), 11.460–488.

3. Zhu Xi, *Zhuzi yulei* [Classified conversations of Master Zhu], ed. Li Jingde (Beijing: Zhonghua shuju, 1986), 126:3037.

4. Zhu Xi, *Zhuzi yulei*, 126.3041.

5. Zhu Xi, *Zhuzi yulei*, 126.3036–3037; 24.587; 126.3030–3031.

6. Zhu Xi, *Zhuzi yulei*, 132.3183.

7. Zhu Xi, *Zhuzi yulei*, 24.587 and 126.3037; see also Qian Mu, *Zhuzi xin xue'an* [A new study of Zhu Xi], vol. 3 (Taipei: San min shuju, 1975), 160–197, passim.

8. Zhu Xi, *Zhu Xi ji*, 74.3894

9. *Lunyu* [*Analects*], Harvard-Yenching Institute Sinological Index Series, supplement no. 16, reprint (Taibei: Chinese Materials and Research Aids Service Center, 1966), 14.24.

10. Zhu Xi, *Zhu Xi ji*, 74.3902.

11. This, of course, is a very general characterization. It should be noted that the *Book of Changes* is more abstract than any of the other Five Classics and more interested in the inner workings of human morality.

12. Respectively, these are *Zhuzi mingchen yanxing lu* [A record of words and deeds of eminent statesmen by Master Zhu], *Yiluoyuanyuan lu* [Records of the origins of the school of the two Chengs], and *Zizhi tongjian gangmu* [An outline of the *Comprehensive Mirror for Aid in Government*].

13. *Taiji tushuo jie* [An explanation of (Zhou Dunyi's) Diagram of the Great Ultimate Explained], *Tongshu jie* [An explanation of (Zhou Dunyi's) Penetrating the Book of Changes, and *Ximing jieyi* [An explanation of (Zhang Zai's) Western Inscription. The names in parentheses within the bracketed translations, here and in note 14, are my addition.

14. *Henan chengshi yishu* [The surviving works of the Messrs. Cheng of Henan], *Henan chengshi waishu* [The supplementary works of the Messrs. Cheng of Henan], and *Shangcai yulu* [A record of (Xie) Shangcai's conversations].

I. FOUNDATIONS OF THE UNIVERSE

1. Throughout his writings and conversations, Zhu Xi uses the terms *li*, *yili* 義理, and *daoli* 道理, which, in order to distinguish among them, I translate as "principle," "moral principle," and "principle of the Way," respectively. They are virtually interchangeable, though Zhu seems to prefer "the principle of the Way" where he is emphasizing principle in its oneness.

2. See Daniel K. Gardner, "Ghosts and Spirits in the Sung Neo-Confucian World: Chu Hsi on *Kuei-Shen*," *Journal of the American Oriental Society* 115, no. 4 (1995): 598–611.

3. Cheng Yi, *Yichuan xiansheng wenji* [Collected literary works of Master Yichuan], in *ErCheng quanshu* [Complete works of the two Chengs], Sibu beiyao edition, 5.12b.

4. Cheng Yi, *Yichuan jingshuo* [Yichuan's explanations of the Classics], in *ErCheng quanshu*, Sibu beiyao edition, 1.2a.

5. Zhu's disciple, Yang Daofu, fl. 1189.

6. *Lunyu* [*Analects*], Harvard-Yenching Institute Sinological Index Series, supplement no. 16, reprint (Taibei: Chinese Materials and Research Aids Service Center, 1966), 17.17.

7. *Zhouyi* [*Book of Changes*], Harvard-Yenching Institute Sinological Index Series, supplement no. 10, reprint (Taibei: Chinese Materials and Research Aids Service Center, 1966), 16, hexagram 24; cf. Richard Wilhelm, trans., *The I Ching, or Book of Changes*, 3rd edition (Princeton, NJ: Princeton University Press, 1967), 505.

8. The *Book of Changes* was originally a divinatory manual consisting of sixty-four hexagrams. Layers of text were added to the hexagrams during the first millennium BCE. To make his case that heaven and earth do, indeed, have a mind-heart, Zhu cites these references from the *Book of Changes*, one of the Five Classics. *Zhouyi*, 21, hexagram 34; cf. Richard Wilhelm, *The I Ching*, 556.

9. Cheng Yi, *Yichuan yizhuan* [Yichuan's commentary on the *Book of Changes*], in *ErCheng quanshu*, Sibu beiyao edition, 1.1a.

10. Zhang Shi (1133–1180), Zhu's friend and influential Neo-Confucian thinker from Hunan.

11. Cheng Yi, *Yichuan jingshuo*, 1.2a

12. Shao Yong 邵雍 (1011–1077) was a major Neo-Confucian philosopher of the Northern Song period.

13. From Jia Yi's 賈誼 (200–169 BCE), "Funiao fu" 鵩鳥賦 [Rhyme-prose on the owl]; cited in Ban Gu 班固, *Han shu* 漢書 (Beijing: Zhonghua shuju, 1962), 48.2227; also translated in Burton

Watson, *The Columbia Book of Chinese Poetry: From Early Times to the Thirteenth Century* (New York: Columbia University Press, 1984), 70–73.

14. "Matter" here is psychophysical stuff that has taken on relatively solid form.

15. Literally, "the yin and yang two psychophysical stuffs."

16. See the section in this chapter titled "Expansive and Contractive Forces of Nature."

17. Shen Gua 沈括 (1031–1095), scientist and statesman of the Song.

18. *Zhouyi*, "Xiaoxu," 9.

19. *Lunyu* 6.22.

20. *Lunyu* 11.12.

21. *Lunyu* 11.12.

22. Based on *Liji* [*Book of Rites*], Shisan jing zhushu [Yiwen reprint] edition, 47.14a.

23. *Zhouyi*, "Xici shang," chap. 4, 40.

24. The solid matter, constituted of the turbid part, is psychophysical stuff as well, but simply not as refined or ethereal as the "clear part."

25. *Huainanzi* [Huainanzi], Sibu beiyao edition, 7.6a.

26. Cheng Hao and Cheng Yi, *Henan Chengshi yishu* [Surviving works of the Messrs. Cheng of Henan], in *ErCheng quanshu*, Sibu beiyao edition, 3.6a.

27. A minister of the state of Zheng.

28. *Zhouyi*, "Xici shang," chap. 4, 40.

29. Cheng Yi, *Yichuan yizhuan* 1.7b–8a.

30. *Kongzi jiayu* [School sayings of Confucius] 4.11a.

31. Zhang Zai, "Zheng Meng," in *Zhang Zai ji* [Collected works of Zhang Zai] (Beijing: Zhonghua shuju, 1978), 19.

32. The goddess of spirit writing. On the Purple Maiden see, for instance, Valarie Hansen, *Changing Gods in Medieval China 1127–1276* (Princeton, NJ: Princeton University

Press, 1990), 76–77; and David K. Jordan and Daniel L. Overmeyer, *The Flying Phoenix: Aspects of Sectarianism in Taiwan* (Princeton, NJ: Princeton University Press, 1986), 38–39.

33. For more on *cheng* and *jing*, see chapters 3 and 5.
34. Xie Liangzuo, *Shangcai yulu* [A record of Shangcai's conversations] vol. 22, Congshu jicheng xinbian edition, 17.
35. *The Zuo Commentary*, in *The Chinese Classics*, trans. James Legge, vol. 5, rev. ed. (Hong Kong: Hong Kong University Press, 1960), 157.
36. Fan Zuyu 范祖禹 (1041–1098) was a prominent statesman and scholar of the Northern Song. Fan's remark here is cited by Zhu Xi in his commentary on *Lunyu* 3.12 in *Lunyu jizhu*, in *Sishu jizhu* [Collected commentaries on the Four Books], Sibu beiyao edition.

2. HUMAN BEINGS

1. For example, Zhang Zai, *Zhang Zai ji* [Collected works of Zhang Zai] (Beijing: Zhonghua shuju, 1978), 374.
2. Zhang Zai, *Zhang Zai ji*, 374.
3. Lü Dalin 呂大臨 (1046–1092) was a prominent disciple of the Cheng brothers.
4. *Lunyu* [*Analects*], Harvard-Yenching Institute Sinological Index Series, supplement no. 16, reprint (Taibei: Chinese Materials and Research Aids Service Center, 1966), 17.2.
5. *Lunyu* 16.9.
6. *Lunyu* 16.9.
7. The *Mean* [*Zhongyong*], chap. 20. References are to standard chapter and verse numbers. See James Legge, trans., *The Chinese Classics*, vol. 1, rev. ed. (Hong Kong: Hong Kong University Press, 1960).
8. *Mencius* 4B.19. See *Mengzi* (*Mengzi yinde*) [A concordance to the *Mencius*], Harvard-Yenching Institute Sinological Index

Series, supplement no, 17, reprint (Taibei: Chinese Materials and Research Aids Service Center, 1966).

9. The *Mean*, chap. 20.

10. Zhu Xi considered Lü to be the author of chap. 8, *Zhongyong jie* 中庸解, from Cheng Yi's *Yichuan jingshuo* [Yichuan's explanations of the Classics], in *ErCheng quanshu* [Complete works of the two Chengs], Sibu beiyao edition. It is to this work that Zhu is likely referring.

11. *Greater Learning* [*Daxue*], chap. 1. References are to standard chapter and verse numbers. See Daniel K. Gardner, *Chu Hsi and the Ta-hsueh: Neo-Confucian Reflection on the Confucian Canon* (Cambridge, MA: Harvard University Council on East Asian Studies, 1986).

12. A reference to *Mencius* 2A.6.

13. *Lunyu* 17.2.

14. Zhu Xi's commentary on *Lunyu* 17.2 in *Lunyu jizhu*, in *Sishu jizhu* [Collected commentaries on the Four Books], Sibu beiyao edition.

15. A reference to *Lunyu* 9.1.

16. *Zhang Zai ji*, "Zhengmeng," in *Zhang Zai ji*, 23.

17. Cheng Hao and Cheng Yi, *Henan Chengshi yishu* [Surviving works of Messrs. Cheng of Henan], Sibu beiyao edition, 6.2a.

18. *Lunyu* 7.38.

19. *Zhouyi*, "Xici shang," chap. 4, 40.

20. *Gewu*, the investigation of things, is a key term in the *Greater Learning*; *qiongli*, probing principle, is Zhu's gloss on *gewu* in his commentary on the *Greater Learning*.

21. A reference to Mencius 2A.6.

22. *Mencius* 3A.1.

23. *Lunyu* 7.30.

24. *Lunyu* 6.7.

25. *Mencius* 6A.8.

26. *Greater Learning*, chap. 1.

27. The *Mean*, chap. 1.
28. Cheng Hao and Cheng Yi, *Henan Chengshi yishu*, 18.2a.
29. *Zhi*, translated here as "will" here, can also have the sense of determination, purpose, or ambition.
30. Cheng Hao and Cheng Yi, *Henan Chengshi yishu*, 24.4a.
31. A reference to *Mencius* 6A.11.
32. *Mencius* 6B.8.
33. *Greater Learning* I.2.
34. *Mencius* 6A.11.
35. Zhu Xi's disciple, Yu Daya (1138–1189), from Jiangxi.
36. *Lunyu* 12.1.

3. LEARNING

1. All are from the *Greater Learning* [*Daxue*], chap. 1. See Daniel K. Gardner, *Chu Hsi and the Ta-hsueh: Neo-Confucian Reflection on the Confucian Canon* (Cambridge, MA: Harvard University Council on East Asian Studies, 1986).
2. Cao Shuyuan (fl. 1190), a disciple of Chen Fuliang (1137–1203), an influential scholar-official from Zhejiang.
3. *Shujing* [*Classic of History*], in *The Chinese Classics*, trans. James Legge, vol. 3, rev. ed. (Hong Kong: Hong Kong University Press, 1960), slightly revised translation here.
4. *Lunyu* [*Analects*], Harvard-Yenching Institute Sinological Index Series, supplement no. 16, reprint (Taibei: Chinese Materials and Research Aids Service Center, 1966), 15.5.
5. *Zhongyong* [*The Mean*], chap. 33. See James Legge, trans. *The Chinese Classics*, vol. 1, rev. ed. (Hong Kong: Hong Kong University Press, 1960).
6. In this passage, Zhu takes *qin* and *gong*, "reverent," to be roughly synonymous with *jing*, "reverentially attentive."
7. Lu Zishou (1132–1180), older brother of well-known philosopher Lu Jiuyuan.

8. A book of Chan monastic regulations in ten chapters and eighty-nine articles compiled in 1103.
9. A reference to *Lessons for Women* by Ban Zhao 班昭 (48–120), who married into the Cao family.
10. The great legendary rulers of China.
11. The Xia (c. 2000–c. 1600 BCE), Shang, (c. 1600–c. 1050 BCE), and Zhou (c. 1050–256 BCE) dynasties.
12. A period of disunion, from 907 to 960, directly preceding the Song.
13. From Zhu Xi's "Preface" to *Daxue zhangju* 大學章句 [The *Greater Learning in Chapters and Verses*], in *Sishu jizhu* 四書集注 [Collected commentaries on the Four Books] (Sibu beiyao edition), 1a–2b.
14. Confucius's grandson and, according to Zhu Xi, the author of the *Mean*.
15. The *Mean*, chap. 33.
16. *Lunyu* 1.1.
17. *Mengzi* (*Mengzi yinde*) [A concordance to the *Mencius*], 4A13, Harvard-Yenching Institute Sinological Index Series, supplement no, 17, reprint (Taibei: Chinese Materials and Research Aids Service Center, 1966).
18. For example, the *Mean*, chaps. 1, 13, 20.
19. The *Mean*, chaps. 19 and 32.
20. These terms are all from the *Greater Learning*, chap. 1.
21. Renowned Chan master, Dahui Zonggao 大慧宗杲 (1089–1163).
22. For example, *Lunyu* 6.27, 9.2, 12.15, 19.6.
23. *Lunyu* 14.35.
24. The first two steps in the self-cultivation process, according to the *Greater Learning*, are the extension of knowledge (*zhizhi* 致知) and the investigation of things (*gewu* 格物). In his commentary, Zhu glosses the "investigation of things" as "probing the principle in things."

25. This is "Supplementary Chapter 5" in the *Greater Learning*. Zhu Xi believed that an original chapter 5 had been lost and so added this passage to the text of the *Greater Learning*. It has been treated by the Chinese tradition as an integral part of the classical text ever since. It is Zhu Xi's classic statement on the extension of knowledge and the investigation of things.

26. *Greater Learning*, chap. 1.

27. The *Mean*, chap. 20.

28. Cheng Hao and Cheng Yi, *Henan Chengshi yishu* [Surviving works of the Messrs. Cheng of Henan], in *ErCheng quanshu* [Complete works of the two Chengs], Sibu beiyao edition, 18.5b.

29. *Henan Chengshi yishu* 3.5b.

30. Reading *ai* 礙 for *yi* 疑 as in Zhang Zai, *Zhang Zai ji* [Collected works of Zhang Zai] (Beijing: Zhonghua shuju, 1978), 321.

31. *Lunyu* 12.1.

4. A THEORY OF READING

1. Zhu Xi, *Zhu Xi ji* [Collected works of Zhu Xi], ed. Guo Qi and Yin Bo (Chengdu: Sichuan jiaoyu chubanshe, 1996), 8.4255.

2. Zhu Xi, *Zhu Xi ji*, 59.3012.

3. Zhang Zai, "Jingxue liku" [Thesaurus of principles for the study of the classics], in *Zhang Zai ji* [Collected works of Zhang Zai] (Beijing: Zhonghua shuju, 1978), 275.

4. Traditional texts sometimes speak of the "Six Classics," a reference to the conventional Five Classics and a sixth one about music that was supposedly lost sometime before the Han dynasty.

5. Zhu Xi, *Zhu Xi ji*, 82.4255.

6. Zhu Xi, *Zhu Xi ji*, 82.4255.

7. Zhu Xi, *Zhu Xi ji*, 59.3012.

8. Zhu Xi, *Zhu Xi ji*, 75.3944–3945. Here the Sage and the Worthy refer to Confucius and Mencius, respectively.

9. From Zhu Xi, *Daxue huowen* [Questions and answers on the *Greater Learning*], in *Sishu daquan* [The complete compendium on the Four Books]. Japanese edition of 1626 based on Yonglo edition of 1415, 20a.
10. Zhu Xi, *Zhu Xi ji*, 54.2728
11. From *Mencius* 6A.8. *Mengzi* (*Mengzi yinde*) [A concordance to the *Mencius*], Harvard-Yenching Institute Sinological Index Series, supplement no, 17, reprint (Taibei: Chinese Materials and Research Aids Service Center, 1966).
12. *Shujing* [*Classic of History*], in *The Chinese Classics*, trans. James Legge, vol. 3, 210, with slight revision.
13. The reference here is not made clear.
14. Written by Jia Yi and copied into the *Han History*.
15. The story of Cook Ding's carving skills is found in chapter 3 of the *Zhuangzi*, (*Zhuangzi yinde*) [A concordance to Zhuangzi]. Harvard-Yenching Institute Sinological Index Series, supplement no. 20, reprint (Cambridge, MA: Harvard University Press, 1956), 7–8. See Burton Watson, trans. *Zhuangzi: Basic Writings* (New York: Columbia University Press, 2003), 45–47.
16. Zhang Zai, *Zhang Zai ji*, 321.
17. *Mencius* 4B.15.
18. *Mencius* 6A.11.
19. *Mencius* 2A.2. See note on page 84.
20. Prominent Zhou dynasty thinkers associated with the school of Legalism, which Confucianism opposed.

5. MORAL SELF-CULTIVATION

1. *Mengzi* (*Mengzi yinde*) [A concordance of the *Mencius*], Harvard-Yenching Institute Sinological Index Series, supplement no. 17, reprint (Taibei: Chinese Materials and Research Aids Service Center, 1966), 6A.8.

2. The *Mean* [*Zhongyong*], chap. 1. See James Legge, trans. *The Chinese* Classics, vol. 1, rev. ed. (Hong Kong: Hong Kong University Press, 1960).

3. The *Mean* I.4.

4. Han Yu, *Zhu Wengong jiao Changli xiansheng wenji* [Collected literary works of Master Changli, collated by Zhu Wengong], Sibu congkan edition, 11.3b.

5. *Shujing* [*Classic of History*], in *The Chinese Classics*, trans. James Legge, vol. 3, rev. ed. (Hong Kong: Hong Kong University Press, 1960), 61–62, with revisions.

6. From Zhu Xi's "Preface" to *Zhongyong zhangju* [The *Mean* in *Chapters and Verses*], in *Sishu jiju* [Collected commentaries on the Four Books], Sibu beiyao edition, 1a–b.

7. *Lunyu* (*Lunyu yinde*) [A concordance to the *Analects of Confucius*], Harvard-Yenching Institute Sinological Index Series, supplement no. 16, reprint (Taibei: Chinese Materials and Research Aids Service Center, 1966), 12.1.

8. The *Mean* 1.5, 27.6, 27.6, respectively.

9. *Greater Learning* [*Daxue*], chap. 1. See Daniel K. Gardner, *Chu Hsi and the Ta-hsueh: Neo-Confucian Reflection on the Confucian Canon* (Cambridge, MA: Harvard University Council on East Asian Studies, 1986), chap. 1.

10. *Classic of History*, James Legge, trans., 61–62, with revision.

11. *Lunyu* 12.1.

12. From Zhu Xi's commentary on *Analects* 12.1, in *Lunyu jizhu* [Collected commentaries on the *Analects*], in *Sishu jiju* 四書集注. Sibu beiyao edition, 8b.

13. From *Liji*, Shisan jing zhushu [Yiwen reprint] edition, 1.8a and 30.23a–b, respectively.

14. *Lunyu* 12.1.

15. The *Mean*, chap. 1.

16. A reference to *Mencius* 7A.3.

17. This paraphrases a comment in Cheng Hao and Cheng, *Henan Chengshi waishu* [Supplementary works of the Messrs. Cheng of Henan], in *ErCheng quanshu* [Complete works of the two Chengs], Sibu beiyao edition, 11.5a.

18. I have not identified him.

Works Cited

Analects. See *Lunyu.*

Ban Gu 班固. *Han shu* 漢書 [History of the former Han]. Beijing: Zhonghua shuju, 1962.

Book of Changes. See *Zhouyi.*

Chan, Wing-tsit. *Reflections on Things at Hand: The Neo-Confucian Anthology.* New York: Columbia University Press, 1967.

Chan, Wing-tsit. *A Source Book in Chinese Philosophy.* Princeton, NJ: Princeton University Press, 1963.

Cheng Hao 程顥 and Cheng Yi 程頤. *Henan Chengshi waishu* 河南程氏外書 [Supplementary works of the Messrs. Cheng of Henan]. In *ErCheng quanshu* 二程全書 [Complete works of the two Chengs]. Sibu beiyao edition.

——. *Henan Chengshi yishu* 河南程氏遺書 [Surviving works of the Messrs. Cheng of Henan]. In *ErCheng quanshu.* Sibu beiyao edition.

Cheng Yi. *Yichuan jingshuo* 伊川經說 [Yichuan's explanations of the Classics]. In *ErCheng quanshu.* Sibu beiyao edition.

——. *Yichuan xiansheng wenji* 伊川先生文集 [Collected literary works of Master Yichuan]. In *ErCheng quanshu.* Sibu beiyao edition.

——. *Yichuan yizhuan* 伊川易傳 [Yichuan's commentary on the *Book of Changes*]. In *ErCheng quanshu.* Sibu beiyao edition.

Classic of History. See *Shujing*.

Daxue 大學 [*Greater Learning*]. References are to standard chapter and verse numbers. See Daniel K. Gardner, *Chu Hsi and the Ta-hsueh: Neo-Confucian Reflection on the Confucian Canon*. Cambridge, MA: Harvard University Council on East Asian Studies, 1986.

de Bary, Wm. Theodore, and Irene Bloom, eds. *Sources of Chinese Tradition*. Second edition. Vol 1. New York: Columbia University Press, 1999.

Gardner, Daniel K. "Ghosts and Spirits in the Sung Neo-Confucian World: Chu Hsi on *Kuei-Shen*." *Journal of the American Oriental Society* 115, no. 4 (1995): 598–611.

———. *Learning to Be a Sage: Selections from the* Conversations of Master Chu, Arranged Topically. Berkeley: University of California Press, 1990.

Greater Learning. See *Daxue*.

Han Yu 韓愈. *Zhu Wengong jiao Changli xiansheng wenji* 朱文公校昌黎先生文集 [Collected literary works of Master Changli, collated by Zhu Wengong]. Sibu congkan edition.

Hansen, Valerie. *Changing Gods in Medieval China, 1127–1276*. Princeton, NJ: Princeton University Press, 1990.

Huainanzi 淮南子 [Huainanzi]. Sibu beiyao edition.

Kongzi jiayu 孔子家語 [School sayings of Confucius]. Sibu congkan edition.

Jordan, David K., and Daniel L. Overmyer. *The Flying Phoenix: Aspects of Sectarianism in Taiwan*. Princeton, NJ: Princeton University Press, 1986.

Legge, James, trans. *The Chinese Classics*. 5 vols. Rev. ed. Hong Kong: Hong Kong University Press, 1960.

Liji 禮記 [*Book of Rites*]. Shisan jing zhushu [Yiwen reprint] edition.

Lunyu 論語 (*Lunyu yinde*) [A concordance to the *Analects of Confucius*]. Harvard-Yenching Institute Sinological Index Series, supplement no. 16, reprint. Taibei: Chinese Materials and Research Aids Service Center, 1966.

The *Mean.* See *Zhongyong.*

Mencius. See *Mengzi.*

Mengzi 孟子 (*Mengzi yinde*) [A concordance to the *Mencius*]. Harvard-Yenching Institute Sinological Index Series, supplement no. 17, reprint. Taibei: Chinese Materials and Research Aids Service Center, 1966.

Qian Mu 錢穆. *Zhuzi xin xue'an* 朱子新學案 [A new study of Zhu Xi]. 5 Vols. Taipei: San min shuju, 1975.

Schirokauer, Conrad M. "Chu Hsi's Political Career: A Study in Ambivalence." In *Confucian Personalities.* Ed. Arthur Wright and Denis Twitchett. Stanford, CA: Stanford University Press, 1962.

Shujing 書經 [*Classic of History*]. In *The Chinese Classics.* Vol. 3. Trans. James Legge. Rev. ed. Hong Kong: Hong Kong University Press, 1960.

Shushi gorui 朱子語類 [Collected conversations of Master Zhu]. Vol. 6 in *Shushigaku taikei* 朱子學大系. Ed. Morohashi Testuji 諸橋轍次 and Yasuoka Masahiro 安岡正篤. Tokyo: Meitoku shuppansha, 1981.

Watson, Burton, ed. and trans. *The Columbia Book of Chinese Poetry: From Early Times to the Thirteenth Century.* New York: Columbia University Press, 1984.

Watson, Burton, trans. *Zhuangzi: Basic Writings.* New York: Columbia University Press, 2003.

Wilhelm, Richard, trans. *The I Ching, or Book of Changes.* 3rd edition. Princeton, NJ: Princeton University Press, 1967.

Xie Liangzuo 謝良佐. *Shangcai yulu* 上蔡語錄 [A record of Shangcai's conversations]. Vol. 22. Congshu jicheng xinbian edition.

Zhang Zai 張載. *Zhang Zai ji* 張載集. [Collected works of Zhang Zai]. Beijing: Zhonghua shuju, 1978.

Zhongyong 中庸 [The *Mean*]. References are to standard chapter and verse numbers. See James Legge, trans. *The Chinese Classics.* Vol. 1. Rev. ed. Hong Kong: Hong Kong University Press, 1960.

Zhouyi 周易 (*Zhouyi yinde*) [A Concordance to the *Book of Changes*]. Harvard-Yenching Institute Sinological Index Series, supplement no. 10, reprint. Taibei: Chinese Materials and Research Aids Service Center, 1966.

Zhu Xi 朱熹. *Daxue huowen* 大學或問 [Questions and answers on the *Greater Learning*]. In *Sishu daquan* 四書大全. Japanese edition of 1626 based on Yonglo edition of 1415.

——. *Daxue zhangju* 大學章句 [The *Greater Learning in Chapters and Verses*]. In *Sishu jizhu* 四書集注 [Collected commentaries on the Four Books]. Sibu beiyao edition.

——. *Zhu Xi ji* 朱熹集 [Collected works of Zhu Xi]. Ed. Guo Qi 郭齊 and Yin Bo 尹波. Chengdu: Sichuan jiaoyu chubanshe, 1996.

——. *Lunyu jizhu* 論語集注 [Collected commentaries on the *Analects*]. In *Sishu jiju* 四書集注. Sibu beiyao edition.

——. *Zhongyong zhangju* 中庸章句 [The *Mean in Chapters and Verses*]. In *Sishu jiju*. Sibu beiyao edition.

——. *Zhuzi yulei* 朱子語類 [Classified conversations of Master Zhu]. Ed. Li Jingde 黎靖德. Beijing: Zhonghua shuju, 1986.

——. *Zhuzi yulei* [Classified conversations of Master Zhu]. Ed. Li Jingde. Chuanijng tang edition, 1880.

Zhu Xi and Lü Zuqian 呂祖謙. *Jinsilu* 近思錄 [Reflections on things at hand]. Congshujicheng edition.

Zhuangzi 莊子. (*Zhuangzi yinde*) [A concordance to Zhuangzi]. Harvard-Yenching Institute Sinological Index Series, supplement no. 20, reprint. Cambridge, MA: Harvard University Press, 1956.

Zuozhuan. [*Zuo Commentary*]. James Legge, trans. *The Chinese Classics*. Vol 5. Rev. ed. Hong Kong: Hong Kong University Press, 1960.

Index